OFFICE SPACE

"A TENANT'S GUIDE TO PROFITABLE LEASING"

By Jack Saltman

To
My Father
Nathan H. Saltman
I'll always cherish the short time we had
together and the lessons you taught me

ISBN 0-9623058-1-2

Published By: The Trinity Publishing & Marketing Group, Inc.
                5415 Lake Howell Road, Suite 123, Winter Park, FL 32792

Library of Congress Cataloging-in-Publication Data

Saltman, Jack.
    Office Space "The Tenant's Guide To Profitable Leasing" / Jack Saltman
    1-800-699-4901

FOREWORD

"Winning is everything" may be a phrase we've all heard, or even felt while cheering for our favorite team. "If you can't stand the heat then get out of the kitchen" is a saying that's supposed to guide us toward being stronger, smarter and richer. We have all been influenced by other catch phrases, fairy tales and even "Gumpisms" ("Stupid is as stupid does"). But what does it take, and where should we go, to find real help, clear advice and solid business savvy?

We all know that experience is the greatest teacher. Both positive and challenging experiences can teach us very meaningful lessons.

In all of my books about self-development, inner fitness, total relaxation and overcoming addictions, there is one common denominator. And that is this: I have learned a great deal from twenty years and tens of thousands of people's experiences. So when people ask me "What makes the *Six Steps to Freedom* so successful when so many other programs have failed?", I explain to them that success in business requires the same common denominator as life's experiences.

Jack Saltman has integrated the knowledge and "how to's" of thousands of experts and decades of his own personal experiences. *Office Space: A Tenant's Guide to Profitable Leasing* is clear, inspiring, creative and practical. His stories are entertaining, enlightening and brilliant. When I sent this book to my real estate co-investors, they wanted to know, "How come there is so much new information that we have never heard before?" They were in the process of renegotiating their own office lease and were able to immediately apply Jack's information and know-how. Success was fast, comfortable, fair and easy. With Jack walking them through each step, they saved thousands of dollars on their transaction.

When I first met Jack Saltman in 1979 at one of his workshops, I knew I wanted to learn more from him. It was obvious he had a special talent for reading between the lines. His business intelligence is open-minded, fair for everyone, and creatively and clearly explained. Every contact I have had with him since then has been helpful to me and positive for my business.

In the pages of this book, Jack Saltman creates a template for intelligent business decisions. Psychologically he is inspiring; emotionally he relaxes everyone with his ability to hold out all of the facts so clearly. In dealing with the complex issue of office leasing, he's a genius.

It is my business to recognize outstanding individuals and their ability to help others. I typically recommend physicians and counselors and do so with full confidence. It is my sincere opinion that in the field of commercial real estate—and specifically in the area of office leasing—Jack Saltman is a hero.

Dr. Brian M. Alman

Brian M. Alman, Ph.D., is a clinical psychologist and hypnotherapist in private practice in San Diego, California. He is the author of Self-Hypnosis: A Complete Manual for Health and Self-Change *and* Six Steps to Freedom: A Simple Plan for Life Control. *Dr. Alman conducts workshops at the Harvard Medical School, the University of California/San Diego, the University of Los Angeles, the University of Hawaii, the Dutch Society of Clinical Hypnosis and several institutions in Europe.*

ABOUT THE AUTHOR

Jack Saltman is president of Compass Investment Properties. He has been a leasing specialist, a commercial real estate broker and a licensed real estate broker since 1977.

In his twenty years of commercial real estate experience, Mr. Saltman has worked for such firms as Cushman & Wakefield, L.J. Hooker International, Jim Wilson & Associates, Olympia & York Southeast, First Office Management and The Galbreath Company. He has leased more than four million square feet of office space and has represented such firms as the Walt Disney Corporation, IBM, Harris Corporation, KLM Royal Dutch Airlines, Stromberg Carlson, Baxter Travenol Labs, Gibco Pharmaceutical, Exxon Corporation and many others.

Long considered an expert—Jack has been quoted or featured in more than 100 national and local newspaper and magazine articles. From 1983 to 1987 Jack Saltman served as chairman of the Market Conditions Committee for BOMA International (Building Owners & Managers Association) and BOMA's Congressional Network. He is a member of the Greater Orlando Economic Development Commission and the Orlando area Chamber of Commerce. He is past president of BOMA/ Brevard and twice-elected vice president of BOMA/Orlando. Most recently Jack has served as president of the Casselberry Little League organization in Casselberry, Florida, where he coached his son Neil and daughter Pam for nearly ten years. Jack's wife of twenty-four years, Risa, has been one of the area's leading residential real estate brokers for the past ten years and currently works with Re/Max Town & Country Realty of Winter Springs, Florida.

Mr. Saltman's leasing experience and industry education has been extensive. He has worked as a tenant representative and as an owner's representative. He has built and run leasing organizations for some of the largest and most successful commercial real estate firms in the United States and in the world. He has acted as a consultant and exclusive or sole tenant representative to some of the nation's corporate elite. Over the years Jack also has actively helped lobby Congress and the EPA on behalf of BOMA and tenants to create consistent legislation for the removal of asbestos in office buildings nationwide. He has addressed local civic groups and national associations on numerous subjects relating to the commercial real estate industry and market conditions.

Jack Saltman is available for instruction, consultations and speaking engagements. He can be reached at 1-800-699-4901.

SPECIAL ACKNOWLEDGMENTS

I received help, encouragement and inspiration in writing "Office Space *A Tenant's Guide to Profitable Leasing*" from many friends and colleagues. I would like to thank my wife Risa, my daughter Pam, my son Neil, and my mother Florence Shaw for their patience, understanding, love and encouragement throughout this project and my life.

To Kevin Jackson, President of Advanced Information Systems Group, a client and a friend who inspired and contributed his time, money and advice in helping me write this book. While working with him on his office space requirement, it was Kevin who said, "I've learned so much you should write a book for tenants and I'd like to be part of it."

I'd like to thank Dan Farmer of Farmer & Baker, Architects for contributing the space plan drawings and "Rule of Thumb for Office Space Planning" in Chapter 4.

Thank you to Henry Chamberlain, Senior Vice President of BOMA International and BOMA International for allowing me to use and refer to 1996 "Standard Method for Measuring Floor Area in Office Buildings," throughout my book.

A special thanks to Charles Figueroa, Office and Industrial Manager of the Hilldrup Moving & Storage Co. United Van Lines, for writing Section II of Chapter 14, "12 Steps to a Successful Office Move."

Thanks to Tom Field of Turner Development for allowing me the use of his company's "Construction Work Letter."

To Jack Snyder, Sheila Morgan, Krishna Prem, Mike and Denise Mullen and others for reviewing, commenting and editing my work. Yes, Sheila, I am grateful you paid attention during fourth grade English.

Thank you to Dr. Brian Alman for writing a fabulous forward and to Max Mogul for bringing me into the Commercial Real Estate Industry.

Thanks to my brother Sheldon Saltman for his guidance, inspiration, encouragement and introductions which helped me get started. And a special thanks to my father-in-law, Mel Alman, for his continued support.

To Ray Cooper and Barney Zick for sharing your guidance, your time, knowledge, contacts and experience with me.

And finally to all the clients I've had the privilege of working with over the years for without you there would be no book at all.

Through the efforts and encouragement of all these wonderful people this project has become a success.

ACKNOWLEDGMENTS

The Standard Method for Measuring Floor Area in Office Buildings, copyright 1996, which is referred to throughout this book and appears in Chapter 3, Section C and in the Glossary of Terms was reprinted with permission from Building Owners & Managers Association, International (BOMA), 1201 New York Avenue, N.W., Suite 300, Washington, D.C. 20005.

The Rules of Thumb for Office Space Planning found in Chapter 4, Section A, and the space plans found in Chapters 8 and 12 were supplied by and reprinted with permission from Farmer & Baker Architects Inc., 601 S. Lake Destiny Rd., Maitland, FL 32751.

The Construction Work Letter in Chapter 12, Section C was supplied by and reprinted with permission from Tom Field, vice president of the Turner Development Co.

Chapter 14, Section B ("12 Steps to a Successful Office Move") is reprinted with permission by Charles Figueroa, office and industrial manager of the Hilldrup Moving & Storage Co./ United Van Lines, 750 Central Florida Parkway, Orlando, FL 32801.

x

CONTENTS

PREFACE

"THE TENANT IS NOT THE PRIORITY, PROFIT IS."
—Anonymous.

Several years ago in South Florida, a major Midwestern developer built an absolutely magnificent high-rise downtown office building, complete with four penthouse apartments. The developer was so impressed with his architectural achievement that he decided in order to successfully lease and manage such a structure, he would have to hire a "heavyweight" from a major market.

The developer turned to his New York office for their recommendation, after all there's no more major market in this country than New York.

They found a "young gun"—the son of one of their New York leasing agents. He interviewed well, made a good appearance, and told of his incredible achievements over his less than five-year career. He was hired and given a very handsome employment package, even by New York standards. The developer moved his new vice president to South Florida, gave him a brand new company car and set him up, rent free, in one of the four magnificent penthouse apartments.

Upon his arrival the new vice president found his office completely staffed with a property manager, two leasing agents and three secretaries. The building was more than 50% leased and occupied by some very impressive tenants. Things went well for the first couple of months; the leasing staff was active, doing deals and were well-liked within the community. The

1

developer was impressed with his new vice president and with the job the South Florida office was doing.

In month three, however, the developer's accounting department noticed that the entertainment expenses for South Florida were extremely high. The new vice president seemed to be entertaining clients five to seven nights a week. Receipts were coming in for dinners at the finest restaurants, including the most expensive wines. There were receipts for breakfast, lunch and even catered parties in his penthouse apartment. Then one day our hero waltzed into work and deposited a pile of bills on his secretary's desk. "I want these to be paid as a building expense," he announced to her. She looked through the bills finding his personal utility bills, phone bills and bills for furniture for his apartment. The secretary walked into his office and said, "I can't do this. These are your personal bills." His reply: "Just do it. Or I'll find someone who will."

His tenants paid for his living expenses and parties for about a year as part of their building's operating expenses—until the developer finally caught on and fired him.

That's one story—all true. Then there's the one about the building owner who hired only maintenance men who were on retirement pensions, so he could keep his payroll down. This owner's philosophy was that 90% of all tenant maintenance problems were imaginary. He just needed a maintenance man who appeared to know what he was doing.

How about the building leasing representative who used to sign side letters to close the lease transaction? He would promise prospective tenants that his company would use their services exclusively if they would lease space in his building. It worked. He pre-leased a building to 82% with three law firms, two architectural firms, three construction firms and two engineering firms. I should qualify my statement that it worked—it only worked until the building opened.

There are thousands of such other stories—some worse than these. The point is that every building owner's profession is to operate and lease commercial properties (office buildings). They have chosen this profession to make a profit and instinctively, good market or weak, building owners will always seek a profit and their employees will sometimes seek their own.

A building owner spends 365 days a year thinking about nothing else. He or she is plotting and planning ways to get you—the prospective tenant—to lease space in their building. The building owner has promised a lender, an investor, or themselves a profit on their investment. The building owner has hired attorneys to write a lease that assures them a profit and protects them from you. The building owner has hired an architect and an engineering firm to design a highly efficient building, insuring a profit from every square inch of the structure and every mechanical device in the building. The building owner has hired advertising agencies and marketing firms to create advertising programs and brochures to lure you into their building at the highest possible price. The building owner has hired corporate officers to oversee the owner's representative who oversees the property manager and leasing director who oversee the day-to-day operations of the property and its staff— all to insure the building owner's profit.

Your only defense is knowledge!

My purpose in writing this book is to inform and educate you—the prospective tenant—for the formidable task you are about to undertake, and to prepare you for the adversary you are about to challenge in his own arena.

CHAPTER 1

DETERMINING YOUR NEEDS

Section I. Personal Needs

Several years ago I was contacted by the vice president of leasing of a very large pharmaceutical company. He was coming to Florida to find locations in Miami, Tampa, Jacksonville and Orlando. Orlando would be his final stop and I was to pick him up at the airport on Thursday morning. "Mel" (we'll call him Mel) told me over the phone that he was looking for approximately 50,000 square feet of warehouse space with a minimal amount of office, a five-year term, and he didn't want to spend more than $4 per square foot. He also said his location preference was the north side of town with easy access to highways. These were his "requirements."

Armed with this information, I was able to find six properties that met his requirements. But since I hadn't yet had the opportunity to spend time with him, I really didn't know his "needs." Because of this, I decided to expand my search by adding a few properties that were less expensive and a few that were of higher quality and more expensive.

On Thursday morning I picked Mel up at the airport. He didn't look so good. He had been on the road since Monday, was tired, anxious to find a property, and then go home. He had caught a cold and was not in great spirits. It was about 9:30 in the morning and he told me he was booked on a 4 p.m. flight back to Atlanta, but he would stay longer if he had to. I assured him that he would be back in plenty of time to catch his flight.

As we left the airport, I suggested we stop for a cup of coffee. Remember, I knew his "requirements" but in order to speed things up I had to know his "needs." Over coffee Mel told me how his week in Florida had turned into a nightmare. He had badly underestimated the cost of space throughout the state. In Miami they wanted $5.75 per square foot while in Tampa and Jacksonville they were asking about $5.25. His entire budget was being "blown out of the water" and he had no idea how he was going to face his boss when he got back. Mel was in trouble and needed a miracle. I thought I might have one.

I told him about a property I had found on the north side of town; it was about a mile from a major highway and it met the rest of his requirements. We could probably get it for less than the $4 he was willing to spend. We were scheduled to see it at 11 a.m.

We visited two buildings I had scheduled for earlier appointments and toured the market a little, acclimating him to the area. The time also gave me the opportunity to learn more about Mel, ensuring that I understood his needs. At 11 o'clock we pulled into the parking lot of the "great deal" I had described to him.

The property was new and the owner was anxious, after all Mel represented a Fortune 500 company. This was a bonus for the owner, who was just hoping for someone who could afford to pay the rent. While doing my research I had learned that the property was 150,000 square feet, totally vacant, and the owner had recently inherited it so he didn't have a lot of money invested in it. The owner's entire motivation was to get the property leased so he could have a steady monthly income. We toured the property, Mel was impressed. I turned to the owner and said, "You're quoting $3.25 right?" Mel's eyes lit up and the owner said, "Well considering the company, I'd take $2.75, providing the build-out works out OK."

6

Mel caught a 2 o'clock flight back to Atlanta. Needless to say, he took the space and more. When Mel arrived back at his office, he reworked his original space requirement for the state of Florida. The 50,000-square-foot requirements for Miami, Tampa and Jacksonville were reduced to 10,000-square-foot distribution points. Orlando was re-designated as the distribution center for the state and Mel leased the entire 150,000-square-foot complex.

This story is not meant to indicate that space is cheaper in Orlando than it is in other Florida markets—sometimes it is and sometimes it isn't. The point is that Mel began his search by addressing his "requirements"—not his "needs." When his requirements couldn't be met in Miami, he accepted the fact that his dollar-per-square-foot estimate was unrealistic. He had it reconfirmed in Tampa and again in Jacksonville. Mel's "requirement" was space; his "need" became quickly apparent once his search began: it was job security and avoiding embarrassment. No one ever asked—and Mel never thought—about his needs, until he came to Orlando.

By addressing his needs, the entire venture became a huge success—and to his company Mel appeared to be an absolute genius.

Section II. Business Needs

Image. Proximity to highways and/or airports. Customer base. Employee retention. Proximity to high-end residential or middle-income residential. Floor plan. Cost. Parking. Downtown vs. suburban. These are just a few reasons why a company might chose to locate in a certain building or in a particular part of town, or even in a certain city, state or county.

Business needs are just as important—and sometimes even

more important—than satisfying your personal needs when it comes to making the best decision of where to locate your business. You must know the type of location and why it would work best for your business. Are you trying to attract new employees? Maybe just keep the ones you have? Does your sales force spend most of its time on the road or in the air? Does your staff take too much time for lunch because of the distance to restaurants?

All these items must be addressed for you to create the perfect scenario.

Section III. The Perfect Scenario

Every successful business, individual or project starts with a vision or dream that successfully transforms itself into a goal.

Your goal is to fulfill your "needs." Notice I did not say your "requirements"—there's a big difference. Requirements are the items needed to fulfill your needs. Your needs are your reasons for selecting a particular location.

Before you begin your search for office space, I would like for you take a few moments to just sit back, relax and imagine the perfect scenario. Visualize the completed transaction as if you were sitting in your new office and everything has gone exactly as you had hoped. Imagine the entire transaction from start to finish—how it all happened, step by step. If you take the time to do this and follow the simple plan set forth in this book, your office leasing experience will hopefully be exactly as you pictured it.

Now that you've taken the time to picture and analyze your needs, it's time to learn something about the people, the places and the language of the world you are about to enter. I know—

you're probably thinking that the next step should be requirements. Well, before we address your office space requirements, it's **absolutely vital** that you fully understand the terminology of the office building business. What you **think** you have agreed to and what you **actually** have agreed to are not always the same.

CHAPTER 2

LEARNING TO SPEAK THE LANGUAGE

Section I. Communicating Your Needs

The typical leasing transaction usually begins with a phone call to a building leasing agent. The prospective tenant tells the agent something like, "I'm looking for 'x' amount of square feet. How much are you charging?" The leasing agent gives a quote such as "$14 per square foot." The prospect sets up an appointment to see the space. The prospect decides, "Gee, that wasn't so difficult," and makes a couple of more calls to other buildings asking the same question and going through the same process.

The prospect sets up appointments to see three buildings all on the same morning. He walks into the first building, goes to the leasing office and the agent brings him directly to a couple of spaces that meet his square footage requirement. As they are touring the building, the agent points out some of the building's amenities, and casually mentions that the common area factor of the building is 15%. A few minutes later he mentions the $14 figure is triple net, there is a charge for after-hours A/C, the expense stop is $4.25, parking is ample at four spaces per thousand, but there's a $45 per month charge per space, and use of the health club will cost him $50 per month per employee.

The prospect starts asking himself, "What happened to $14 per square foot? What's 'triple net'? What's a common area factor? Is an expense stop an additional charge?"

11

Our prospect moves on to buildings two and three only to find more confusion. One is talking about full service, another is talking about tenant improvements and upgrades, annual bumps, CPI, mullions, usable vs. rentable square footage. It all started simply enough. What are they now talking about?

Trust me, it's simple. Let's just run through some of the key terminology you must know and understand while touring an office building.

Section II. Terminology

After Hours Usage. Tenant's need for additional working hours beyond the normal operating hours for the building as set forth in the lease. Typically, if tenants require after-hours utility usage, they will pay an additional, agreed-upon fee.

Americans with Disabilities Act (ADA). Federal legislation passed in 1990 requiring employers and business owners to make "reasonable accommodations" to facilitate employment of the disabled.

Annual Operating Expense Increases/Overages. A charge passed onto the tenant representing the tenant's proportionate share of building operating expense costs greater than the amount agreed upon in the original lease (referred to in lease as "expense stop" or "base year expenses"). When an owner refers to the building's "expense stop" as $4.50, this simply means that the first $4.50 of building operating expenses are being paid by the building. If the building operates at a higher rate—let's say $5 per square foot—you will pay the difference between $5 and $4.50, or an additional 50 cents per square foot. When an owner quotes you on the "base year basis," he is saying that you will pay the difference between the amount the building operated at in the base year and its current operating expense cost. An example would be "base year of 1996." Let's say the building operated at $6 per square foot in 1996, and operates at $6.50 in 1997. You would pay the difference of 50 cents per square foot in 1997.

Base Rent. The rate at commencement of the lease.

Base Year Operating Expenses. The amount the owner is paying to cover the cost of operating the building in a given year (for example: "base year 1996 expenses" would reflect the cost to operate the building in 1996.) In subsequent years you would pay the difference in the amount it costs to operate the building based on the percentage of the building you occupy.

BOMA Method of Measurement. Generally accepted throughout the office building industry as the standard and fair method of measuring office space. Some landlords use other methods, including their own. (See "Glossary of Terms" in back of book.)

Building Amenities. Features of the building that add to the comfort of the tenant while in occupancy (for example: coffee shop, health facility, covered parking, breakrooms, conference rooms, express mail machines, etc.).

Building Improvements. Any improvements made to the overall appearance or comfort of the building (for example: new carpeting, painting, upgrade of elevator cabs, etc.).

Building Operating Hours. The normal hours of operation for the building as set forth in the lease.

Build-Out. Refers to the construction of the tenant's proposed space to make it ready for occupancy; or, to comply with tenant's construction needs according to the terms and conditions of the lease. Also referred to as "T.I." (tenant improvements).

13

Class A Building. Commonly used when referring to the highest quality buildings. Building classification may rate how the building is generally accepted in the market, or could be a personal classification by the individual referring to that structure.

Class B Building. Used to describe an average building. Building classification may rate how the building is generally accepted in the market, or could be a personal classification by the individual referring to that structure.

Class C Building. A term commonly used to describe a below-average building. Building classification may rate how the building is generally accepted in the market, or could be a personal classification by the individual referring to that structure.

Commencement Date. The actual date the lease takes effect.

Common Area. Any space in a building affording common use for all tenants, such as lobbies, corridors, restrooms, building breakrooms, building conference rooms, health facility, janitorial closets and storage rooms. This excludes "vertical penetrations" (see Glossary of Terms) such as stairwells and elevator shafts. There are times when the common area of a building is much greater than the amount competitively acceptable in the market. In such cases the building owner may quote a common area factor much lower than the actual percentage. This is done for the building to remain competitive and leasable in the market.

Common Area Factor. A percentage of the building determined by the building owner to represent the total amount of space in the building affording common use for all tenants such as lobbies, corridors, restrooms, building breakrooms, building conference rooms, health facility, janitorial closets and storage rooms. This excludes "vertical penetrations" such as stairwells and elevator shafts.

CPI (Consumer Price Index). Usually used as the basis for adjusting annual rent increases. It is also referred to as a "cost of living increase."

First Right of Refusal. A right given to the tenant stating that before the landlord will lease the space in question, (usually expansion space), the tenant will be given the right to lease it first. The first right of refusal is usually negotiated into the lease and is typically governed by an agreed upon time limit.

Free Rent. A period of time given to the tenant by the landlord to occupy the space before having to commence paying rent. Usually done during extreme soft periods in leasing when the market is known as a "tenant's market."

Full-Service Lease. In some markets referred to as a "gross lease." Covers the cost of rent, electricity and janitorial service. Does not include phone expenses, furniture, moving services, etc. This terminology is sometimes used when landlord should be quoting the type of lease as a "modified gross lease." (Tenant and landlord share operating expense cost).

Lease Term. Number of months or years the agreed-upon lease will remain in force.

Leasing Agent. The individual assigned the responsibility, usually by the building owner, to lease out the property.

Month-to-Month Lease. An agreement by landlord and tenant to allow the tenant to occupy space on a month-to-month basis. Typically this type of lease can be terminated by either party with a thirty-day notice.

Monthly Rent. One-twelfth of the annual rent paid to the landlord usually on the first of the month.

Net Lease. A lease that is not all-inclusive. For example, the lease agreement indicates the tenant will pay for their own janitorial service and electrical service. Or, the lease indicates tenant will pay separately for both janitorial and utilities.

Operating Expenses. The cost to operate the property. For example: real estate taxes and assessments, utilities, insurance, maintenance and repairs, common area refurbishing, janitorial services, materials, supplies, repair service, cost of property management, security fees, employees and contractors, outside maintenance, cost of signs, rubbish removal, pest control, bulb replacement, etc.

Operating Expense Pass-Throughs. The amount that is passed onto the tenant in order to operate the building. This would represent any amount over and above the amount agreed to in the lease; referred to as "base year expenses" or the "expense stop." This amount would be proportionate to the percentage of space occupied by the tenant.

Pro Rata Share. Percentage of building occupied by the tenant. Usually based on the rentable or leasable square footage measurement of the tenant's space compared to the rentable or leasable square footage of the building.

Quoted Rate. The rate per square foot that is quoted to prospective tenants when inquiring about the property. May or may not be negotiable. This may be quoted on a "rentable" or "usable" basis.

Rentable Square Footage. The amount of square feet, including the common area factor of the building. This typically is the square footage the tenant will pay rent on.

Tenant Improvements. Usually refers to the improvements done to a space to make it ready for the new tenant's occupancy. It can also mean improvements being done by a tenant.

Tenant Improvement Allowance. This is the amount of money the landlord is willing to contribute for the build-out of the tenant's space. It is usually quoted as "x" amount of dollars per rentable or usable square feet.

Tenant Representative. Any broker or representative exclusively representing the rights of a tenant during the course of a transaction.

Turn-Key Build-Out. A completed build-out of space, ready for the tenant to move into. It is a term that's used loosely, usually relating to all-inclusive tenant improvement costs.

Usable Square Footage. The amount of square feet measured within the confines of the tenant's space.

The terminology and definitions in this list are meant to be simple and generic for most office markets. There will be an occasional twist or different interpretation from market to market. Take the time to familiarize yourself with most of these terms and they'll save you dollars and heartache—and keep you in control of the transaction.

You don't have to memorize this list, but do become familiar with these terms. You'll find a more complete list of terms related to the commercial real estate and specifically the office building phase of the business in the Glossary of Terms in the back of the book.

CHAPTER 3

MARKET KNOWLEDGE

Section I. Controlling Your Own Destiny

The key to making a good deal is being able to identify one.

Now that you're armed with a plan (you know your "needs"), and you can speak and understand the language of the office building industry, it's vital that you understand the health and condition of your local **commercial real estate** market. That's right, I am stressing the word **commercial** real estate as opposed to **residential** real estate.

All too often people casually scan their local newspaper and read about real estate sales being strong or weak and assume the reference is to the overall industry of real estate. Not true. Conditions governing each aspect of real estate are usually quite different.

These differences also hold true within the commercial real estate market itself. For instance, lenders may feel there's a high demand for industrial space in a particular market, but little to no demand for office space. Therefore, they will willingly lend money for the construction of new warehouses, but not for new office buildings. The same holds true for apartment complexes and hotels. If the demand exists in one area as opposed to another, and times are reasonably good, the type of property showing strong demand and low supply will usually reap the benefit.

The following conditions will dictate whether you're dealing with a *landlord's market* or a *tenant's market*. If the inventory of office buildings in a given market or sub-market is more than 90%, and there's little to no new construction in progress, you can bet you're in a landlord's market. If there's an abundant supply of office space available and lots of new buildings under construction, you are in a tenant's market.

Market conditions don't change overnight, but they do have a tendency to repeat themselves. I'm a firm believer that history is our greatest teacher, especially in the study of market trends. This, I believe, is one of the reasons why most landlords prefer to write leases on a three- or five-year basis (in some markets they'll go ten years, but that's unusual). The term of a lease is a gamble on both sides, depending on where you believe the cost of office space will be going over the next few years.

Remember: knowing your market does not mean you have to become an expert, just a knowledgeable consumer.

Section II. Sources of Market Knowledge

If you know you'll be looking for office space in the near future, I would suggest researching the following sources:

1.) Local Newspapers. Read your local newspaper's business section regularly, looking specifically for stories related to office buildings, the office building market and its trends, as well as any legislation or major corporate moves or layoffs that may have a direct effect on the industry. Research back issues for charts, market research reflecting trends, prices and comparisons of buildings and sub-markets.

2.) Local Business Journals. If there is a local business journal in your area, look for articles related to the office building industry. Research back issues as you would newspapers looking for charts, market research reflecting trends, prices and comparisons of buildings and sub-markets.

3.) Local Office Guides. These publications not only carry valuable tips on office space hunting, furnishing, etc., but they also usually list the majority of buildings in your area. These lists are typically broken down by sub-market, and supply such information as name of building, size of building, cost-per-square-foot of space, and name and phone number of the leasing contact person. (Check this source anytime prior to your search).

4.) Local Magazines. These publications will generally carry stories about the local office building industry. (Check six months to a year in advance of your search.)

5.) Economic Development Commission. This group, which in some markets is referred to as the Industrial Development Commission, is charged with attracting industry and growth to the community. They should have the most up-to-date information on the market. They may also be able to give you information regarding tax breaks, economic development zones, etc. Quite often incentives are made available—in the form of tax breaks, cash bonuses, flexible zoning ordinances and more—to attract businesses to a particular state, county, city or sub-market. These incentives are not always exclusive to large firms, and by taking advantage of such incentives could make your move a profitable one.

6.) Local Chamber of Commerce. A good source for general information about the area. Chambers will most likely refer you to good sources as well as members in the commercial real estate industry such as brokers, developers and building owners.

7.) Local Chapter of BOMA (Building Owners & Management Association). This source can put you in touch with knowledgeable people within the industry. You should ask for any market information they may have as well as a list of members to contact.

8.) Local Chapter of NAIOP (National Association of Industrial & Office Parks). Another excellent source that can put you in touch with knowledgeable people. You should ask for any market information they may supply as well as a list of members to contact.

9.) Commercial Brokerage Firms. Most of the commercial brokerage offices do extensive market research in order to remain competitive within the market. This is a perfect opportunity to become acquainted with the brokers in your community. I suggest contacting four or five brokerage firms in your market to ask questions and discuss your needs. Gather as much market information as you can and become acquainted with the broker or person you'd be working with—that is, if you decide to use a broker. Once you do this, when it comes time to decide whether or not to use a broker, you'll know who to call, based on knowledge, compatibility and philosophy.

10.) Building Leasing Agents Within Your Sub-market of Interest. Call at least six buildings within the sub-market of interest to you. Not only can you obtain the information you need on their building, you could also discuss the condition of the sub-market in total.

11.) Local Public Library. This is always a good source for newspaper and magazine articles. Some even carry local market office studies.

The purpose of your research is to determine five crucial issues:

1.) The Condition of the Market. Will I be looking for office space in a landlord's or a tenant's market?

2.) Ideal Location. Where should I locate my office: downtown vs. suburbs? High-rise vs. low-rise, north or south of town, office park or free-standing facility?

3.) Price Range. What is the rental range I can expect to pay for my space? Are the rates quoted on a full service or net basis? How is full service defined in this market?

4.) Standard Market Practice for Handling Operating Expense Increases, Annual Rental Increases & Common Area Factors. Can I expect any surprises or hidden costs because of practices that are generally accepted in this market?

5.) Parking or Amenity Fees. Is it standard to charge for parking or other amenities in this market?

Once these questions are answered, and the answers properly applied in the lease negotiation process, 90% of your post-lease surprises will be gone.

TENANT'S MARKET STUDY

Building Name	Address	SF:Rentable	Vacant	%Occ.	Rate	Services	Factor	Expenses	Built	Leasing Agent	Phone
Westville Center	1266 Lk Wilson Dr.	38,000	24,400	35%	12.50	Full	12%	$6(BY96)	1976	Jerry Vincent	(407) 699-7771

Section III. How Did They Come Up
With That Figure?

Probably the most confusing and complex aspects of leasing office space is figuring out how much square footage you need and understanding how the landlord or building owner came up with that figure.

On the surface, measuring office space appears to be pretty straightforward: Length multiplied by Width equals Square Feet. Well that's the formula, but there's a lot more to it.

This is the aspect of renting office space where you really have to understand some terminology and how these terms are applied. Let's review some of these terms:

Bay Depth. The distance measured from the building corridor to the outside window or wall.

BOMA's Method of Measurement. Generally accepted throughout the office building industry as the standard and fair method of measuring "usable" and "rentable" square footage. To determine the "usable area" of your space, measure from the inside finished surface of the corridor wall and the dominant portion of other permanent walls (i.e. exterior walls; dominant portion could be glass) to the center of the wall that separates your office from the adjoining office. Columns and interior walls will not be deducted from the measurement. To determine the "rentable area" of your space, first determine the rentable area of the floor by measuring to the inside finished surfaces of the outer building (outer glass to outer glass that makes up the exterior walls of the floor). Remember—it's Length multiplied by Width equals Square Footage. When measuring, exclude any vertical penetrations such as stairwells and elevator shafts. Before you determine your percentage of "common area" or "loss factor" of your floor, you must determine the "usable area" of that floor. Do this by taking the "rentable" measurement and subtracting areas of common use to the tenant (i.e. corridors, restrooms, utility closets, janitorial closets, common conference room, and other building amenities located on that floor). To determine your "rentable area," "usable area" and "common area factors," apply the following conversion formulas:

Rentable Area ÷ by Usable Area = Rentable/Usable Ratio

Usable Area X by Rentable/Usable Ratio = Rentable Area

Rentable Area ÷ by Rentable/Usable Ratio = Usable Area

Common Area Factor or Load Factor. Percentage of space in a building affording common use to all tenants. Does not include vertical penetrations such as stairwells and elevator shafts.

Common Area Maintenance Fee (CAM Recovery). Additional charge passed onto the tenant for maintaining the building's common areas.

Demising Wall. The wall that separates one tenant from another.

Dominant Portion. A feature that makes up more than 50% of the inside surface of a permanent wall.

Finished Surface. A wall, ceiling or floor (including glass) that has been placed in the leased office space for the tenant's use.

Gross Square Footage. The total square footage of the building. Measured from the outside walls and includes the basement and all vertical penetrations of the building.

Leasable Square Footage or Rentable Square Footage. The amount of space in the building or within the tenant's space once the common area or load factor has been added to the measurement. It is typically the amount of square footage on which your rental rate is based. Usable Square Footage + Building Load Factor = Leasable or Rentable Square Footage.

Pro Rata Share. Percentage of the building occupied by the tenant.

Usable Square Footage. The amount of space found within the tenant's immediate space, with no add-ons.

Vertical Penetrations. Areas that serve more than one tenant such as stairs, elevator shafts, flues, pipe shafts and vertical ducts. For measurement purposes, these items are not deducted if their purpose is to serve only one tenant.

Office space measurement is probably the most important single issue when leasing office space. It is the one item that everything in your agreement hinges on. It dictates the size of your space, the cost of your space, the basis for increases and pass-throughs.

Office space measurement is also one of the truly great unsolved mysteries of commercial real estate. It seems, even in following guidelines, that no two people measure space the same exact way. It is the one great area of contention in leasing space.

Over the years I have tracked the progress and growth of the Orlando office market through building specific charts. These are charts that list individual buildings in the market. I update these charts every three months and it always amazes me how entire office buildings can grow and shrink in size over such a short period of time. How does this happen? An office building is a pretty solid structure. Once it's been built to certain square footage specifications, it can't change—can it?

Well, I refer to this phenomenon as the "Theory of Evolution."

When the square footage of a building is quoted, it is usually done on a rentable or leasable basis, not the gross square footage. Remember, rentable or leasable is the basis on which you will be paying rent. Gross square footage is the overall size of the building. Let me explain how the building is measured, according to the BOMA Standard of Measurement.

1.) Gross Square Footage. This figure is arrived at by measuring the outside dimensions of each floor then adding the total square footage of all these outside floor dimensions.

2.) Rentable or Leasable Square Footage. This is determined by measuring the inside of the building's exterior walls then deducting the vertical penetrations of the building and totaling the rentable square footage of each floor. This is the square footage typically quoted as "building size" for leasing purposes.

3.) Common Area Factor/Load Factor/Loss Factor. This is the percentage of the building that is common and available to all tenants in the building (restrooms, corridors, lobby, suites used as building amenities, janitorial closets, storage closets, elevator, electrical or storage rooms).

4.) Usable Square Footage. This is determined by subtracting the amount of common area from the rentable square footage of the building.

Back to my "theory of evolution." In some cases the quoted size of the building (in rentable square footage) can be effected by renovations being done to common areas, or by the landlord's reduction of the quoted common area factor due to a disproportionate amount of lobbies, corridors, or other building amenities. In most cases the change is caused by re-leasing and constant remeasurement of individual space within the building.

When you tell a leasing agent the amount of square footage you're looking for, he or she will usually refer to a list or chart (sometimes called a vertical leasing plan) to check vacancy and square footage availability. This plan is usually updated as the space is leased, showing who is in occupancy, which spaces are vacant and the square footage of these spaces. These leasing plans are usually passed down from generation to generation. If they are not consistently updated with each new transaction, their accuracy is questionable. It is important that you confirm the amount of square footage you're leasing by requiring the space be remeasured by an architect or some other specialist in this field.

CHAPTER 4

CONVERTING NEEDS TO REQUIREMENTS

Section I. How Much is Too Much?

Without knowing measurement techniques, which I'll address later in this book, it probably seems difficult to make this determination but it isn't. There are a few rules of thumb that can get you started.

The standard office is usually based on an estimate of 150 to 200 square feet per person, plus 10% to 15% for flow. Law firms, accounting firms or any business with unusual requirements such as law libraries, multiple conference rooms, or oversized reception areas are obviously not your typical office user. They would estimate a much higher square foot per person basis. They also would have to be aware of floor load capacity (how much weight a floor can handle per square foot) because of such things as libraries and extensive file requirements. On the opposite end of the spectrum would be a reduction in this per person approach for firms that need extensive open-floor planning. These could possibly be insurance offices, real estate offices, travel agencies or even district or regional sales offices for larger firms.

One of the most common errors is estimating office needs on a five- or ten-year plan and leasing the maximum amount of space called for in the plan. Why pay rent on 5,000 square feet when you're currently using only 1,500 square feet? Rent the 1,500 you currently need and as part of your lease, negotiate an option or first right of refusal on additional space. Remember: landlords make their money by leasing space. It's highly unlikely they're going to object to your firm taking additional space at a later date. It's also highly unlikely that if you have leased too much space, they'll take it back.

Be aware that when you opt for additional space in your building, landlords typically try to tie your expansion of space into an extension of your lease term. There are several reasons for this. If you expand, obviously the landlord will most likely be contributing additional dollars towards the build-out of your expansion space. Therefore, a longer lease term means more rental income and helps justify the additional dollars being spent on your expanded space. Secondly, if they can get you to add term to your lease under the same conditions set forth in the original lease document, then you've agreed to a higher overall effective rate for the remainder of the lease. Remember—if you add a year or two to the end of the lease, your increases in rent and operating pass-throughs continue at a higher rate.

Here's another money and space-saving tip that may help. While touring prospective buildings, pay close attention to amenities such as building conference rooms, coffee shop or cafeteria, and storage closets—areas available to tenants at lower cost or no cost. If a building offers these kind of amenities, you may find you don't need a conference room, a break area or all that high-cost storage area in your own office.

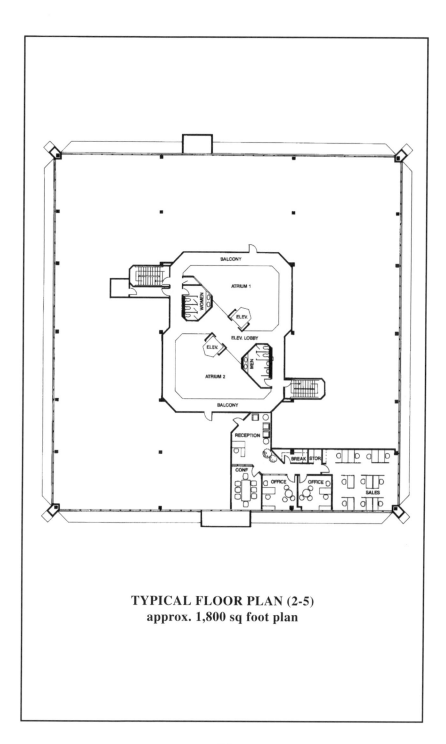

TYPICAL FLOOR PLAN (2-5)
approx. 1,800 sq foot plan

33

RULES OF THUMB FOR OFFICE SPACE PLANNING

A. Typical President's Office or Chairman of the Board– 250 to 400 s.f.

B. Typical Vice President's Office–150 to 250 s.f.

C. Typical Executive Office (Executive Secretary, Manager or Administrative Assistant)–100 to 150 s.f.

D. Partitioned Open Space–50 to 100 s.f. (Clerical Manager or Supervisor)

E. Open Space–50 to 100 s.f. (Secretary or Clerk space)

F. Conference Rooms –Allow minimum of 15 s.f. per person for theater style or classroom seating, allow 30 to 35 s.f. per person for conventional conference seating.

G. Workroom–Approximately 8' to 9' in width. This includes 30' counters against each wall with a 4' aisle between. Length depends upon the number of people working in the room and the amount of mail activity.

H. Reception Room– Including Receptionist and seating for 2-4 people: 150-250 s.f.
Including Receptionist and seating for 6-8 people: 250-350 s.f.

I. File Room–Allow for approximately 7 s.f. per file. Suggested aisle width varies from 3' to 4'. Minimum is 2'8".

J. Library–Allow 12" for book shelves against walls. 24" for back to back shelving. Aisle space minimum is 2'8", with seating for 4-6 people, 175-450 s.f.

K. Employee Lunch Rooms–Allow 20-30 s.f. per person, not including kitchen. Kitchen and serving area should be a minimum of 1/3 to 1/2 of the dining room.

L. Clerical Pool Area– Allow 80-100 s.f. of usable area per person.

M. Corridors and Circulation– 20%-25% of the total usable areas for executive offices, reception rooms, open clerical areas, conference rooms, libraries, file, mail and storage rooms, computer rooms. Suggested corridor widths are 5' for principal office corridors, 6' for public corridors, 3'8" to 4'6" for secondary interior corridors. Clearance between desks should be at least 3'. Suggested width of corridors in which secretaries are located: 10'. This allows for a standard 5' long secretarial desk and 5' passageway which is a comfortable width for two people. Minimum for this type of corridor is 8'.

N. Coat Closets– Allow 1 linear foot for 4 coats—3" per person.

O. Water Coolers/Drinking Fountains–Allow a minimum of 1 unit per 75 people or as directed by applicable codes.

P. Standard Door Sizes– Standard office door is 3' x 7'. Double entrance doors are 6' wide (two 3' doors).

Information provided by Farmer & Baker Architects, Inc.

Section II. Location, Location & Bang for the Buck

The most crucial and most sensitive decision you will make during the entire lease process is "Where should I locate my business?"

Not only will you select a location, but you may well be determining the personality of your entire company and who you will be doing—or not doing—business with. I'll even go as far as saying that location in some cases can determine whether or not your business will grow or even survive.

When I first established my commercial leasing brokerage in the mid-1980s, I was offered space at no cost provided I located my office on-site. I was given the exclusive right to lease the property. The building was magnificent. It was located in the heart of a rapidly growing suburban office park in the north Orlando area and gave me everything I was looking for: price, location and image. My firm quickly developed the reputation as the "outstanding north suburban leasing brokerage in town."

Sounds great doesn't it ? It wasn't. My plan was to be the "outstanding leasing brokerage in town"—not just in the north part of the city. The location I had selected had dictated my corporate image. Prior to opening my firm, I had been generally considered an authority on the overall Orlando market. My choice of locations had changed the way my prospective clients and the community viewed me. It changed the nature of my business and even changed my original business plan.

My original plan had called for slow deliberate growth— one office to cover the entire market. By locating approximately five miles north of downtown (the central business district), I not only had my image changed, but I found myself out of the day-to-day flow of market information. I had to work harder to maintain market knowledge. Instead of interfacing with those in the know on a daily basis, I was making phone calls trying to keep up with the latest market trends. I quickly secured another building, as an exclusive, in a south part of town. Once again the owner offered me an office, rent-free. I took it and immediately staffed the office. My image changed again and my firm became viewed as "the outstanding suburban leasing brokerage in town."

I did ultimately end up with a downtown location, but it took three years. By that time I had hired fourteen employees and had secured more than 1.7 million square feet of space under exclusive right-to-lease agreements.

The point of my story is simple. I could have initially controlled my own destiny by paying a little rent, and realizing that location had an impact on my company's image and ultimately its future. My first office location should have allowed me to control my image, stick to my original game plan, and ultimately would have given better control over my firm's growth.

Here are some factors to consider in choosing the right area for your firm:

1.) Business image
2.) Customer base
3.) Information base
4.) Supplier base
5.) Employee base
6.) Employee retention
7.) Location image
8.) Building image
9.) Easy accessibility
10.) Building can be easily found the first time.
11.) Safety of area
12.) Area amenities
13.) Length of commute
14.) Delays during peak traffic hours
15.) Accessibility to public transportation
16.) Cost of space

You are almost ready to enter the market. Keep in mind that right now you are looking for six to twelve buildings that would generally fit your plan. At this point you are searching for general information. You will narrow your search to a handful of buildings during your tour of the various sub-markets.

Section III. Renewing Your Lease or Finding New Space?

When you're facing the decision of whether or not to move, the normal question becomes: "Should I renew or find new space?" So, let's now take a look at lease renewal.

To the landlord, lease renewal is the result of good property management. To the tenant, lease renewal is the time to correct past errors and oversights or to move on.

I have found that most landlords would like to keep their current tenants, and most tenants would like to avoid the inconvenience and expense of having to move. If the initial lease process was carefully conducted and completed by both parties, and their relationship has been an amicable one, then there is no reason to believe that the lease renewal process should be any different. There are, however, always exceptions to the rule.

Typically the landlord will contact the tenant six months to a year prior to the termination date of the tenant's lease and propose terms for renewal. The advantages for the landlord are obvious. If the tenant renews, the landlord most likely is not going to have to invest a lot of tenant improvement dollars to keep the tenant in the space. In most cases the landlord isn't paying the high commission rates to an outside broker, or to a staff, that he or she had to pay to get the tenant in the first place.

The advantages to the tenant should be equally as obvious. The tenant won't have to pay moving costs for relocating nor will the tenant have to go through the entire process of finding new space to lease. Plus, the renewal process affords both parties the opportunity to correct any mistakes they may have made in the original lease.

Now that I have stated the "obvious," let me warn you: some landlords view the renewal process as an opportunity to take advantage of the "obvious."

You are about to enter another agreement that will require some further negotiation. A lease renewal will extend your tenancy in the same building for probably another three to five years. So ask yourself: How was your *first* three to five years?

I then strongly recommend that tenants, who are thinking about renewing, review their business plan and their needs for the upcoming three to five years. How efficient is the space you are now occupying? Will you need to expand or reduce? Does the property still portray the image you want for your firm? Has the building lived up to your initial expectations? How responsive has management been to your needs? How responsive and effective is building maintenance? Were there any unpleasant surprises you have experienced since occupying? What is the current condition of the office market?

Once you've looked at your personal and business needs for the upcoming three to five years, start doing a little market research. Go back to some of the original sources you used during your initial search for space to see how and if things have changed and where the experts see things heading. Call several buildings that are competitive with the one you now occupy. Ask questions about rates, tenant improvement allowances, concessions, operating expenses and annual increase rates.

Even if you have decided to stay where you are, arm yourself with as much market knowledge as you can muster—you're going to need it!

Your next step is to review your lease. Look for items you may have overlooked in your initial negotiations. Then, look for areas that need to be updated. Your base rent, the base year being used to adjust your operating expense increases, annual percentage of increase, expansion options, renewal options, occupancy and expiration dates, etc.

Here are some things to watch out for in your landlord's renewal proposal:

*1.) **Rental rates continuing to increase from your current rental rate.***

BEWARE: That $15 rate you signed on your original deal five years ago, with 4% annual increases, is now $17.55. So, $17.55 would be your current rental rate. The market may dictate that new tenants coming into your building are paying less.

*2.) **Non-adjustment of "base year expenses" or your "expense stop" figure.***

BEWARE: Anything over the amount reflected in your lease or renewal is what the landlord is passing through to you as your proportionate share of excess operating expenses. Excess is over and above the base year figure or expense stop figure.

If there is something that needs attention in your space—carpets cleaned or replaced, new paint or wall covering, a wall moved or any other space adjustment—ask for it now. If it's not in the lease or any of its attachments, it doesn't exist. Make sure you are being offered a new tenant improvement allowance and be sure to use it to improve your business image. Remember—a new tenant would get it.

If you are happy with where you are and everything is in order, then make your adjustments to the landlord's proposal and set up a meeting to negotiate your changes. Negotiate as if you were negotiating the terms of your original lease. This transaction is a binding adjustment to the original lease and you will have to live with its results for the next three to five years.

Always build a case to move—it may justify the reason to stay. Moving can have positive effects such as improved corporate image, more efficient space layout, improved employee morale, reduced costs, more accessibility to customers, and many things you didn't consider when you first moved in. Building such a case also strengthens your negotiating position and gives you a back-up in case you are not satisfied with your landlord's renewal terms.

Section IV. The Sublease & the Lease Assignment

The Sublease

Sublease situations usually occur when a company has to move before its lease expires. Reasons can vary from company mergers, downsizing or upsizing, headquarters is closing local or district offices, or companies are going out of business. Subleases can be a great opportunity for start-up companies, firms with less than strong financial statements, temporary space needs, or companies that need additional space during certain times of the year.

The sublease is actually a three-party agreement, and in most leases the landlord reserves the right to approve the subleasee. The landlord will almost always keep the original tenant liable under the terms of the original lease. This protects the landlord's position since the landlord most likely has not had direct dealings with the subtenant. It also insures the landlord continued receipt of rent. Some leases even stipulate that the tenant will not be allowed to charge in excess of the tenant's rental payment. Or, that if an additional amount is charged to the subtenant, the landlord and the tenant will divide the profit.

Since the sublease is a three-party agreement, the subleasee must not only agree to the terms and conditions of the tenant's lease, but must also follow any terms and conditions agreed upon by the tenant and landlord. Payment of rent is normally continued to be made to the landlord by the tenant, while the subleasee will pay rent to the tenant.

If you're a tenant thinking about subleasing your space, it is important you understand that this may be a costly transaction. On the surface it may appear to be a simple transfer of space, allowing you some financial relief by having another party pay the rent. But in reality you might be incurring some heavy additional expenses. If someone were to come along and assume your position immediately, with no adjustments to the space, consider yourself lucky. In order to sublease your space you may have to hire a broker, and you may have to reconstruct the space to meet your subtenant's needs. While this process of leasing and construction is going on, you're still obligated to continue paying rent to the landlord. Make sure you understand the whole picture before you decide to sublease.

If your arrangement with the subtenant is that they pay rent directly to the landlord, it would be a good idea to protect yourself in the original lease agreement by making sure there is a provision allowing you to stay in the space and continue paying the landlord rent, in case your subtenant were to default.

If you're in the market to lease space as a subleasee, you are leasing space from someone or a company that considers this space to be a financial burden. This presents an excellent opportunity for a company with less than perfect credit or one that is just starting up. This also sets up conditions for making a very good deal. It can also be a great way to get into a better building at a lower cost.

The Lease Assignment

A lease assignment differs from the sublease in that the liability and direct obligations to the landlord are assigned to another party, although the landlord still tries to keep the original party responsible under the original terms and conditions of the lease.

Assignments are quite common when one company buys another or when ownership is transferred from one partner to another.

CHAPTER 5

DO YOU NEED A BROKER?

Section I. The Role of the Commercial Leasing Broker

Now that you've taken the time to educate and prepare yourself, it's time to make another important decision: *"Should I use a commercial leasing broker?"*

It's important that this decision be made **now**. Most real estate brokers are commissioned sales people. Their primary source of income stems from completing your transaction. One of the most common mistakes made by the prospective tenant is realizing too late that he or she needs a broker. Or that they need a broker for all the wrong reasons. If you are going to choose a broker, you naturally want his or her full attention and dedication to help you achieve your goal of making a good deal. If you have decided to work with a broker, choose one **now**, before you start looking for space.

Let me tell you about Jerry, a client of mine. Not too long ago, Jerry called me and said, "Jack, I need your help. I'm expanding to about 7,000 square feet. I'd like to stay in my building, but my landlord isn't being too helpful. Everytime he makes an offer, he withdraws it. I've been trying for three months to make a deal with him but I'm not getting anywhere. My current agreement is a month-to-month. Will you help me find space in another building?"

I set up an appointment with Jerry and told him I'd take care of it.

45

I met with Jerry the following Wednesday and we discussed his situation. Jerry still wanted to stay in his building—if he could. He indicated his landlord was being unrealistic in how much he was asking. Jerry based this on a proposal he got from the building next door.

Now from a broker's perspective, let's take a look at what has happened to my motivation. Jerry just told me his first choice is to stay where he is. His second choice is to move next door. Not only has he visited the building next door, but he has already negotiated a preliminary deal without me. The odds of my making any money on this deal are pretty slim. There's no commission, so why did Jerry call me?

It's simple. Jerry wanted me to change his mind by finding him the ultimate space—an office that was so good and at such a great price that he'd have to take it. From my perspective, as a broker, this deal is a long shot. If I can move him, I'll make $25,000. If I can't, I get nothing. My answer to Jerry: "Sure I'll help you." The reality though is that I'll give it a shot, but I'm not going to spend a lot of time on this. The prospect will probably stay where he is. In a case like this, the odds are against me.

But I was fortunate. Jerry and I openly discussed his needs and my needs. I explained the broker's position and the gamble he was asking me to take. Jerry wasn't aware of my position. He immediately offered to pay me for my time as a consultant, whether he decided to stay or move to the building next door.

Jerry ended up staying because he felt the timing of space availability in the alternate building just wouldn't work. He had felt, because of timing, that he had no choice but to renew and expand in his current location.

I chose this particular story because it illustrates two of the most common mistakes made by prospective tenants when entering the leasing market or looking to renew or expand their current space. If you are going to use a broker, make that decision before you enter the market on your own. Be aware that in some buildings and in some markets, building owners either pay brokers no commission or pay dramatically reduced commissions on renewals and expansions. In Jerry's case, he had gone as far as opening negotiations with a landlord and then called me for help. Had Jerry called me in the beginning, and worked with me exclusively, the transaction would have been done more quickly and efficiently. He would have had my total commitment and wouldn't have lost three months worth of time, money and aggravation by allowing his landlord to play games with him.

Sometimes, even if your choice is to remain in your current building, it's worthwhile to look at alternative locations. Many times you may get more perks on a new lease than you would on a renewal. It gives you the opportunity to upgrade your corporate image, and at worst it gives you more leverage in dealing with your own landlord if his initial renewal proposal isn't particularly aggressive. Don't wait until it's too late to have a backup proposal. Just as people check their worth in the job market by looking for a new job, you should check the lease market to see if you can get a better deal. Looking at alternative office space is like the mate who has wandering eyes. They're only making sure that they have the best.

Take a look at some common mistakes made by prospective tenants in dealing with a broker:

1.) Visiting prospective buildings before hiring a broker.
2.) Working with multiple brokers.
3.) Not interviewing several brokers before hiring one.
4.) Not understanding that a tenant representative is working for the tenant.

5.) Not understanding that the building leasing agent works for the landlord.
6.) Thinking that using a broker will increase the lease rate.
7.) Allowing a broker to control the deal—the tenant should control the broker.
8.) Not educating oneself to the market before hiring a broker.
9.) Not understanding that the broker is a commissioned salesperson motivated by dollars.
10.) Not realizing that a broker is capable of performing more than 200 real estate functions.

QUALIFYING
YOUR PROSPECTIVE
LEASING BROKER

1. Firm Name: _____

2. Broker's Name: _____

3. Firm's Address: _____

   _____

4. Firm's Telephone Number: _____

5. Firm's Fax Number:_____

6. Scope of Firm: International_____   National_____
   Regional/Statewide_____   Local with Network_____
   Affiliation_____   Local Unaffiliated_____
   Other_____

7. Type of Firm: Commercial_____   Residential_____
   Other_____

8. Number of Offices: Internationally_____   Nationally __
   Regionally_____   Statewide_____   Locally_____

9. Firm's Years in Business_____

10. Firm's Years in Business in the Local Market_____

11. Number of Brokers Locally_____

12. The Firm's Reputation is Based on its Strength in:
   Residential Sales_____   Office Building Sales_____
   Retail Sales_____   Industrial Park Sales_____
   Office Building Leasing_____   Retail Leasing_____
   Industrial Leasing_____   Hotel/Restaurant Sales_____
   Business Brokerage_____   Commercial Land Sales_____
   Residential Development Land Sales_____
   Residential Land Sales_____   Other _____

49

13. When Leasing Space Does the Firm Specialize in:
Tenant Representation_____ Building Representation___
Both_____

14. If the Firm Handles Building Representation, How Much
Space is Currently Under Exclusive Agreement?
Commercial Office____sq.ft. Industrial Space_____sq.ft.
Retail Space____sq.ft.

15. How much Space is: Downtown____sq.ft.
Suburban____sq.ft.

16. Broker's Field: Commercial_____ Residential____

17. Broker's Specialty: Commercial Office Leasing_____
Industrial Leasing_____ Retail Leasing_____
Land Sales_____ Office Building Sales_____
Industrial Sales_____ Hotel/Restaurant Sales_____
Business Sales_____ Other _____

18. Does the Broker Handle: Tenant Representation_____
Owner Representation_____ Both_____

19. What Percentage of His/Her Business is Done in:
Tenant Representation____ Owner Representation____

20. How Long Has the Broker Been in the Commercial Real
Estate Business? _____

21. How Long Has the Broker Been Specializing in a Particular
Field of Expertise? _____

22. What Brokerage Firms has the Broker Worked for Within
the Commercial Real Estate Industry: _____

_____

_____

_____

23. What Firms has the Broker Represented that You Might Recognize_____

24. What is the Largest Transaction the Broker has Ever Handled? _____

25. What is the Smallest Transaction the Broker has Ever Handled? _____

26. What is the Smallest Transaction the Broker Would Consider Working With Now? _____

27. What Transaction is the Broker Most Proud Of and Why?

_____

_____

28. Have the Broker Describe What He or She Envisions His or Her Responsibilities are as Your Tenant Representative.

_____

_____

29. Have the Broker Describe What He or She Envisions as a Good Deal. _____

_____

_____

30. Ask for the Name and Number of the Five Most Recent Transactions the Broker has Worked On (Not successfully concluded, simply worked on), and Ask the Broker's Permission to Contact These People.

   1. _____

   2. _____

   3. _____

   4. _____

   5. _____

31. Conclude the Interview and tell the Broker You Will Be in Touch.

Section II. Choosing the Right Broker

When you choose a broker, you are buying that person's time, knowledge and commitment.

A leasing broker can be anything from a tour guide to a deal maker and negotiator— it's your call. Your decision should be based on your self-confidence, your time availability and above all your faith in your broker's knowledge and ability.

If you have done your homework (as suggested in Chapter 3, "Market Knowledge"), you already will have been in touch with several brokerage firms in your area asking for market information. Once you've taken this step, you're well on your way to choosing a broker that you will be comfortable with. This should give you a base of five or six people to interview.

Other methods of finding leasing brokers are:

1.) Referral
2.) Repeat business with a former broker.
3.) Recommendation by the local Economic Development Commission.
4.) Using sources quoted in newspaper articles or other publications.
5.) Networking acquaintances
6.) Hiring a broker that has met you on a cold call.

Three methods I strongly recommend:

1.) Doing business with a broker you've worked with previously and are comfortable with.
2.) Working with one of the brokers who shared their market knowledge with you.
3.) Talking with friends and other business people about good brokers they have worked with in the past and recently.

In all cases I urge you to interview carefully before hiring. Yes, I did say "hiring." Although in most markets this individual will be paid by the owner or landlord of the property, he or she is actually *working for you.* Once you have selected your leasing broker, that person is now a tenant representative. You are the prospective tenant and they have accepted the position of representing your best interests in this transaction.

While interviewing, keep your needs and the current conditions of the market in mind. You are looking for someone who is compatible with you and the people you'll be dealing with. You need a person who knows the current condition of the market and how it got there. This person must also have a handle on the most recent transactions being done in the market and know how and why they were done. Most importantly, you're looking for someone who portrays the proper image of your firm.

Section III. Brokers to Avoid

1.) Aggressive Brokers. Too often people are impressed with brokers that have the reputation for being aggressive. More often than not, this will work against you. If your need is for the "thrill of the kill," by all means this broker is for you. The aggressive broker always tries to beat up the opposition, wearing them down until they've reached their objective: a steal. The aggressive broker always thinks that they've squeezed the deal for all it's worth. In reality, they lose and ultimately, if you are their client, you lose, too.

When they do achieve their objective—which is rare—they have hurt the landlord, the building and all the tenants in that building, including you. If the landlord has buckled to more than one of these aggressive brokers, he's in trouble and has to find a way to offset those losses. This offset could result in reduction of services, poor maintenance, understaffing, higher operating costs, etc. Usually the aggressive broker loses, but thinks he has won. He or she walks away with huge concessions for their client and returns to the client to brag about the deal. In reality, he walked away with giveaways that the owner built into the deal for just such an occasion, and nothing more. Plus, some owners won't deal at all with this type of broker.

2.) The Selective Broker. Some people like to work with the "elite" element of the industry. Don't mistake the "prima donna" for a member of the elite. This broker has his or her own set of special rules. He's doing you a favor by fitting you into his busy schedule. You'll know him right away—he'll end up interviewing *you.* Your business might be too new, your space requirement too small, or perhaps he works with only Fortune 500 companies, or large credit worthy tenants.

3.) The Inexperienced Broker. Some people choose a broker based on the company he or she works for and not their qualifications. The inexperienced broker is the one who is going to learn by making mistakes. Everyone does and that's OK, but I'm sure you would rather he get his education at someone else's expense. This broker is usually hired when the interviewing process is not used, or when someone has hired a company and not an individual.

4.) The One-Dimensional Broker. This is the broker who understands only one side of the transaction, or one aspect of the business. This individual has experienced the business from only one side. He or she has been only a broker, or has worked for only a property owner. It's difficult to see both sides of the transaction when you haven't experienced both sides. If you choose to work with this individual you will undoubtedly have his total commitment, but a very limited perspective of the entire transaction and its long-term effects.

A word of caution: *some* landlords and *some* brokerage firms have a tendency to play the condition of the market for all it's worth. For instance, when the market is weak for the landlord and strong for the tenant, *some* brokerages will not deal with a landlord until they have negotiated an exceptionally slanted commission agreement in their favor. It stresses that payment of their commission be based on full commission paid; not only on the initial transaction but also on your renewals, expansions and even a full commission if you should purchase the building at some time in the future. The agreement insists they be paid a full commission even if they are not directly involved in that transaction. You, the tenant, will not be brought to that property until the landlord agrees to the broker's terms. This is obviously a strong-arm tactic that favors only the broker, not the landlord or you, the prospective tenant.

When the market heavily favors the landlord, *some* landlords will offer the broker commission on the initial transaction only with no commission to be paid on the tenant's renewals or expansions. These landlords usually will take a hard line when negotiating with you on such issues as caps and controls on rental increases, operating expense pass-throughs, tenant improvement allowance dollars and other items. The quoted rate usually will be higher and the negotiated terms of the lease will be tougher on the tenant, keeping the lease heavily in favor of the landlord and giving few or no concessions. If you are thinking of renewing your lease under these conditions, you may find yourself paying a higher rental rate than a new tenant. The landlord may take the approach that you will stay because it is going to cost you too much to move.

I hope the above examples of brokers help stress the importance of the interview in choosing a representative that is compatible with your personality, your needs, and the existing market conditions.

Section IV. The Dangers of Using Multiple Brokers & the Letter of Tenant Representation

Recently I was sent a referral by a residential real estate broker. Her husband worked for a major telecommunications company and his division had been notified that they would have to move from their present company-owned site. The requirement was for 12,000 square feet and the manager was told he had approximately eight months to find space and move.

During the Monday morning staff meeting, the manager made the announcement that he had been directed by the home office to find new space. Over the next couple of days he was approached by several staff members saying they knew brokers who could make his task a bit easier. The manager suggested they have their brokers contact him so he could interview them and decide which one to use.

I contacted the manager immediately upon receiving the referral and set an appointment to meet with him the next morning. I must admit I was a little skeptical about the legitimacy of the requirement. This particular tele-communications company had its own real estate department with a division locally. It was unusual that one of its divisions would look for space without first clearing it through their own real estate people. Nevertheless I decided to meet with the manager as scheduled and would address this concern during our meeting.

We met the next morning. I found the division manager very pleasant, very open and honest, but through his own admission, totally inexperienced at finding office space. I expressed my concern about his operating independently of his real estate division. He assured me that he had been directed by his superiors in Atlanta and New Jersey to find space on his own. After discussing his needs and requirements, I asked for a letter, signed by an officer of the corporation, indicating exclusive representation of his company regarding this transaction. He indicated that he was working with another broker as well, a friend of one of his department chiefs, and couldn't give me a letter of exclusive representation. I then asked for a letter indicating that I was representing his company exclusively on the properties I would be presenting to him. He agreed and delivered this letter just prior to our initial visit to the properties. Once I had protected my position, I asked if the other broker had indicated the properties he intended to show him. The manager mentioned two that I knew wouldn't work. I set an appointment with him to look at a few buildings. My experience told me that there were only two or three potential buildings that would work for him. I registered his company, as my client, with these properties.

We toured the buildings I felt he'd be interested in. They were perfect. The division manager supplied me with a space plan, indicated his building preferences, and asked me to request lease proposals from each property.

The manager returned to his office and called the other broker to thank him for his time and inform him that his services were no longer needed. He had found two buildings that worked well for his needs. The broker pleaded for an opportunity to show him just a couple more buildings that would work so much better than the ones he liked. Since the manager didn't want to hurt anyone's feelings, he agreed. The next morning the other broker showed up at the manager's office with an agreement for the manager to sign. The manager asked about the agreement, the broker assured him it was merely an agreement allowing him to represent the company on the properties he was about to show him. The manager was familiar with this type of agreement, after all he had just had his boss, an officer of the corporation, write and sign a similar letter for me. He signed it and they were on their way.

The next day I got a call from the other broker. He told me my services were no longer required by this company. He indicated that the manager still liked the properties I had presented but the manager had signed an exclusive agreement with him, now making him the company's sole broker in this transaction. I asked for a copy of the agreement, which was faxed to me immediately.

I called the manager and told him about the call I had just received. He was shocked. "How can he do that?" he asked. I asked him about the agreement he had signed. He said, "He told me it was merely to protect him on the properties he was showing us." "Didn't you read it?" I asked. "No, I trusted him. I'll straighten this out."

A couple of days later I received a call from the company's real estate department. Due to corporate downsizing, this division no longer had an office space requirement. They were being merged with another division and would be housed in another corporate facility. "Thank you for your efforts" the person told me.

The other broker sued for commission.

The manager was so concerned about "hurting someone's feelings," that he did himself a disservice. The transaction would have gone smoothly had he interviewed the brokers, selected one and agreed to be exclusively represented by one of the two brokers.

Most landlords and building owners require brokers to present authorization from the company they represent in a given transaction. This authorization should be given to the broker in writing. Its purpose is to avoid confusion and legal conflict for everyone involved. It is vital if you have not written this authorization yourself, that you read and fully understand the document you are about to sign.

It is not my intent to tell you that you need to use a commercial leasing broker. My intent is simply to point out the positives and negatives of such a decision and ultimately how it will effect your transaction.

CHAPTER 6

PREPARATION FOR THE BUILDING VISIT

Section I. Preview the Area

It's now time to look for office space. You are now prepared, you understand your needs and requirements, and you have a general idea of locations that will work best for your business. Let's talk about your mind-set and your approach.

It is important you understand that you are about to enter into a long-term relationship. For the next three to five years of your business life you will be virtually living in the building you choose, with people you haven't met yet. The commitment you are about to make is like getting married, with no way out for the first three to five years. Obviously you need to find an attractive building run by compatible people.

I suggest you bring along a camera. Taking pictures may help you remember details about the buildings you are about to visit. Video cameras are especially useful in helping you recall every detail of your visit.

You've done your research and have a pretty good idea of how much you want to spend and a general idea of where to locate. It's now time to take a ride—or even a walk—and look at several areas that fit your price range and location needs.

Be sure the area is what you have envisioned. Look at the proximity of restaurants, hotels and retail. If the area is suburban housing, is it middle-income, high-income or low-income? This could be where your employees will be drawn from—where they now live. What's the proximity to airports and/or highways? Is it close enough to your customers or supplier base? Is it convenient to where you live or want to live?

Look at a few of the buildings in the area. Are they attractive and well-maintained? Are the grounds appealing? Is there enough available parking? How far will you or your customers have to walk from car to building? Does the initial appearance of the building portray the image you envision for your company?

You've found several buildings of interest. Let's go inside:

	Yes	No
Does the building have security ?	___	___
Is the lobby warm and appealing?	___	___
Atrium lobby?	___	___
Standard lobby?	___	___
Is the lobby impressive?	___	___
Is the lobby clean?	___	___
Are the lighting fixtures in working order?	___	___
If there's a fountain, is it working?	___	___

Check the tenant roster:

Do I know any tenants in the building?	___	___
Are most of the tenants major corporations?	___	___
Are most of the tenants local companies?	___	___
Are any of my competitors here?	___	___

Check the Restrooms:	Yes	No
Are they clean ?	____	____
Are they attractive?	____	____
Are they well-supplied?	____	____
Are they conveniently located?	____	____
Are they handicapped equipped?	____	____

OK, that's it. The first step is done. Now you can take the information you've gathered, go back to your office, home or hotel room, and review your findings.

Section II. The Phone Tour

You are about to speak to two important people associated with the prospective property: the receptionist and the building's leasing agent. If they are pleasant and your call seems important to them, you are off to a good start. If they are rude and you're an inconvenience to them—BEWARE!

Introduce yourself, state your square footage requirement and when you would like to occupy. Ask if they have it or will have it available. If your requirement is such that you must be on a particular floor or need to be near the elevators, let them know. Find out how many spaces they have that would fit your needs.

Ask about the rental rate and if it may differ according to location in the building. Ask if the rate they are quoting is based on gross, modified gross or net terms. Ask about the building's parking ratio and if they charge for parking. Does the building have covered parking and is parking on-site or off-site? Finally, ask about the building's common area factor, its vacancy rate, operating expenses, and how they handle pass-throughs to their tenants.

Once you feel comfortable that you have enough information and you still feel you would like to visit the building, set up an appointment. I would repeat this process until you have about five or six buildings to visit. Any more than six can become confusing.

Do not stop in without an appointment! It puts both you and the leasing agent at a disadvantage. He or she hasn't had time to prepare for your visit, and most likely you haven't gathered enough information to take the next step.

QUESTIONS TO ASK WHEN CALLING FOR INFORMATION ON THE TELEPHONE

1.) "I'm looking for "x" amount of square feet for a particular month move-in. Do you have it available?"

2.) "Where in the building is the available space located?"

3.) "What's the price per square foot?" _____

4.) "Is that quote rentable or usable?" _____

5.) "Is your lease full service?"_____

6.) "What does that include? _____

7.) "What length lease will you entertain?" _____

8.) "What's the 'common area/loss factor' of the building?" _____

9.) "What is your parking ratio?"
_____ per _____sq.ft.

10.) "Is your parking on-site or off-site?" _____

11.) "Is parking free or is there a monthly fee?" _____

12.) "How much are your operating expenses?" _____
"How are they handled in your lease?" _____

13.) "What kind of amenities does the building offer?"

14.) "When would you be available to show me the building?"

There are many questions that can be asked but I suggest you keep the phone conversation as brief as possible. Get just enough information to decide whether or not a tour of the building is worthwhile.

CHAPTER 7

THE BUILDING VISIT

Section I. The Preliminary Tour

As you interface with the individuals involved in this process, it is important to remember that you are seeking a *long-term relationship*. The initial impressions of all parties will carry on throughout if this is the building you choose.

I am talking about the all-important *first impression*. This gives you an opportunity to judge the building and the people who will play an important role in your business life over the next three to five years. It also gives the leasing/management staff of the building the opportunity to determine if you are the type of person—and the type of business—that will make a good "fit" for their building.

All building tours start differently. Sometimes there is no building tour at all if it's in the pre-construction stage. For the purpose of this book, let's assume there is a building. And, for the purpose of discussion we'll say the building was built in 1986, so we're dealing with "second generation space." This means the building has little or no new space. All the office suites within this building vary in size and have been occupied at one time or another.

You have arrived at this prospective building on time for your appointment. The receptionist/secretary greets you enthusiastically and by name. She informs you the leasing agent has been expecting you as she escorts you into the conference room and offers you a seat and a cup of coffee. Not bad, huh?

A moment later the building leasing agent enters the conference room and greets you with equal enthusiasm, also by name. He takes a seat while saying, "Let's take a couple of minutes to just chat. I'd like to be sure I fully understand your needs." He asks some questions about your business, your industry and about you. He then asks, "If you were to select my building as your new business address, could you describe for me your vision of the ideal space and describe the perfect transaction, so that I can try to meet your needs." You spend about five or ten minutes answering his questions. Now he knows what he has to do to meet your needs, and make a deal with you. He also knows that your business fits his building's needs and that you're the kind of person he can live with throughout a long-term relationship. You are now ready for a tour of the building.

I've just described the best-case scenario, which unfortunately doesn't usually happen. Let's go to the other extreme:

During the 1980s, I was fortunate enough to represent one of the most influential companies in Orlando while securing in excess of 250,000 square feet of office space throughout the Orlando office market. This particular requirement was for approximately 5,000 square feet of downtown retail/office space. My client wanted a class A building in a class A location. We had already toured two of the nicer buildings in the downtown area and had a 1:30 p.m. appointment at a third building. We arrived on time for our appointment. When I approached the receptionist, she had her back to us and was talking on the phone. She looked over one shoulder and put up a single finger, and returned to her phone conversation, back still turned, never acknowledging us as she continued her conversation for another five minutes. When she finally acknowledged us, we were informed that the leasing agent hadn't returned yet from lunch, but he'd probably be back soon, have a seat.

Fifteen minutes later, in strolled the leasing agent with his bosses. No apology, simply "I'll be with you in a couple of minutes." Had class A downtown office buildings been more plentiful in Orlando at the time, I'm sure my client would have stormed out, but there were only three buildings that met their criteria, so we waited. A few minutes later the leasing agent reappeared and invited us into the conference room. As we sat at the large conference table, he walked over to the television set in the front of the room and inserted a videocassette. That was it. My client stood up and said "We've been here for over half an hour waiting to see office space, not a movie. Either show us the space or we're gone." The leasing agent insisted on showing the movie. My client stormed out.

Although this is an extreme example of arrogance, I've seen it occur all too often. There isn't a building in existence that is nice enough to offset arrogance by its leasing staff, management staff or its ownership. Remember: you're the customer and you deserve to be treated with dignity and respect. Such acts are indicative of how a long-term relationship might be. You'll be stuck with these people for three to five years. How will they respond when problems occur?

CHECKLIST FOR YOUR BUILDING SEARCH

Building Location
- [ ] Downtown
- [ ] Suburban
- [ ] Office Park
- [ ] Free-Standing
- [ ] Close to Highways
- [ ] Close to Airport
- [ ] Close to Customers
- [ ] Close to Suppliers
- [ ] Close to Home
- [ ] Close to Employees' Homes
- [ ] Close to Hotels
- [ ] Close to Restaurants
- [ ] Close to Shopping

Building Age
- [ ] Currently Under Constr.
- [ ] Newly Constructed
- [ ] (Under one year)
- [ ] Five yrs. old or less
- [ ] Ten yrs. old or less
- [ ] Fifteen yrs. old or less
- [ ] Twenty yrs. old or less
- [ ] Rehab. or Historical Bldg

Initial Impression of Building
- [ ] Class A Building
- [ ] Class B Building
- [ ] Class C Building
- [ ] Well-Maintained Grounds
- [ ] Availability of Employee Parking
- [ ] Availability of Customer Parking
- [ ] Availability of Disabled Parking

Building Characteristics
- [ ] High-Rise (Over 10 stories)
- [ ] Mid-Rise (3-10 stories)
- [ ] Low-Rise (1-2 stories)
- [ ] Over 500,000 sq.ft.
- [ ] Over 200,000 sq.ft.
- [ ] Over 100,000 sq.ft.
- [ ] Over 50,000 sq. ft.
- [ ] Over 30,000 sq.ft.
- [ ] Over 10,000 sq.ft.
- [ ] Under 10,000 sq.ft.
- [ ] Multi-Tenant Building
- [ ] Single-Tenant Building

Building Site Advantage
- [ ] High Visibility
- [ ] Easily Located by Visitors
- [ ] Landmark Building
- [ ] Landmark Location

Building's Amenities & Features
- [ ] Atrium Lobby
- [ ] Efficient Lobby
- [ ] Well-Maintained Lobby
- [ ] Well-Maintained Interior
- [ ] Landscaping
- [ ] Well-Maintained Floors
- [ ] Clean Bathrooms
- [ ] ADA modifications in place
- [ ] Well-Maintained Elevators
- [ ] Response of Elevators

70

Section II. Touring the Building

Since you've already previewed the building during your initial tour of the area, this will give you a second opportunity to check how well the property is maintained. As you approach the building, recheck the outer conditions of the building, the parking lot, landscaping, outside signage and trash. This could reflect your company's own image.

You will find an additional checklist at the end of this chapter to further help you tour the property. Now you are ready to meet the building leasing agent and tour his or her property.

Here is a list of questions for you to ask:

1.) "How does the property quote square footage? Are they quoting 'usable' or 'leasable/rentable'?"

2.) "What is the building's 'load factor'/'common area factor'?"

3.) "Is the lease full-service? Net? Modified gross?"

4.) "Can you meet my desired occupancy date?"

5.) "How long will it take for you to secure a building permit?"

6.) "How long for the construction of the space?"

7.) "Are there any problems I should know about, such as asbestos, radon, or the use of fiberglass in the building's ducting?"

8.) "What kind of tenant improvement allowance is typically offered? Is that being quoted on a 'rentable/leasable' or 'usable' basis?"

9.) "How long are the bay depths?" (Important for layout of your space.)

10.) "What's the percentage of building occupied?"

11.) "What kind of businesses already occupy the building?"

12.) Re-ask about the rate per square foot.

13.) "Is property management on- or off-site?"

14.) "Is building maintenance on- or off-site?"

15.) "How often are janitorial services performed and what does that include?"

16.) "Is there day maid service available for emergency clean-up?"

17.) "Is there space planning available? Who pays for it?"

18.) If space planning is available; "How many changes am I allowed on the initial plans?"

19.) "Is the expense of the initial space planning deducted from tenant improvement allowance?"

20.) "What is the distance between window mullions?"

21.) "Are window blinds or window treatments included?"

22.) "Are there restrictions on blinds, curtains or window treatments?"

23.) "How is the building zoned for A/C and heat?"

24.) "Am I able to control my own A/C and heat?"

25.) "What are the standard building operating hours?"

26.) "Do I have access to my space after hours? How do I access the building after hours?"

27.) "How do my customers access the building after hours?"

28.) "Do you charge for after-hours use of utilities? How much?"

29.) "Any recent problems with security in or outside the building?"

30.) "Is your parking lot well lit for the employees' safety?"

31.) "What is the building parking ratio?"

32.) "How often and where is mail delivered?"

33.) "What's the location and freight elevator policy?"

34.) "Does the building have a loading dock?"

35.) "Is parking free or do we have to pay?"

36.) "Is your parking located on- or off-site?"

The following is a list of items to recheck during your tour of the property:

1.) Condition of elevator cabs

2.) Responsiveness of elevators

3.) Cleanliness of stairwells

4.) Cleanliness of restrooms

5.) Condition of the building's common areas such as corridors, carpeting, walls and lighting.

6.) Consistency of door numbering

7.) Conditions of tenant entry doors

8.) The overall general appearance and upkeep of the building

Once you have taken the building tour, it's time to thank the leasing agent for his or her time and let them know you'll be in touch. Move onto your next scheduled tour.

When you have completed all your tours and building visits, it's time to analyze the data you've gathered. If you're comfortable with two or three of these buildings, rate them in order of preference.

If you find, after touring these buildings, that only one or none of the buildings meet your needs, you'll have to go back into the market to find additional suitable alternatives. When you begin negotiating, it's always best to have a primary and a secondary backup in case negotiations break down.

CHECKLIST
WHEN TOURING BUILDINGS

Building Location

☐ Downtown
☐ Suburban
☐ Office Park
☐ Free-Standing
☐ Close to Highways
☐ Close to Airport
☐ Close to Customers
☐ Close to Suppliers
☐ Close to Home
☐ Close to Employees' Homes
☐ Close to Hotels
☐ Close to Restaurants
☐ Close to Shopping

Building Characteristics

☐ High-rise (over 10 stories)
☐ Mid-rise (3-10 stories)
☐ Low-rise (1-2 stories)
☐ Over 500,000 sq. ft.
☐ Over 200,000 sq. ft.
☐ Over 100,000 sq. ft.
☐ Over 50,000 sq. ft.
☐ Over 30,000 sq. ft.
☐ Over 10,000 sq. ft.
☐ Under 10,000 sq. ft.
☐ Multi-Tenant Building
☐ Single-Tenant Building

Building Age

☐ Currently Under Construction
☐ Newly Constructed (Under 1 yr.)
☐ 5 Yrs. Old or Less
☐ 10 Yrs. Old or Less
☐ 15 Yrs. Old or Less
☐ 20 Yrs. Old or Less
☐ Rehab. or Historical Building

Building Site Advantage

☐ High Visibility
☐ Easily Located by Visitors
☐ Landmark Building
☐ Landmark Location

Building's Initial Impression

☐ Class A Building
☐ Class AA Building
☐ Class B Building
☐ Class C Building
☐ Well-Maintained Grounds
☐ Availability of Employee Parking
☐ Availability of Customer Parking

Building's Amenities & Features

☐ Atrium Lobby
☐ Efficient Lobby
☐ Maintenance of Lobby
☐ Condition of Interior Landscape
☐ Condition of Flooring
☐ Cleanliness of Bathrooms
☐ ADA Modifications in Place

Building's Initial Impression (Cont)

☐ Availability of Disabled Parking
☐ Availability of Covered Parking
☐ Parking Ratio 2 spaces per 1,000
☐ Parking Ratio 3 spaces per 1,000
☐ Parking Ratio 4 spaces per 1,000
☐ Parking Ratio 5 spaces per 1,000
☐ Parking Convenient to Building
☐ Free Parking
☐ Paid Parking
☐ Outer Appearance of Building
☐ Parking for Delivery Vehicles

Building's Amenities & Features (Cont)

☐ Condition of Elevators
☐ Response of Elevators
☐ Availability of Freight Elevator
☐ Availability of Building Loading Dock
☐ Quality of Tenant Roster
☐ Building Security
☐ Coffee Shop
☐ Health Club
☐ Building Retail Shops
☐ Building Operating Hours

OTHER FACTORS TO CONSIDER

☐ Price Per Square Foot
☐ Lease Terms
☐ Cost of after-hours use of utilities
☐ Full Service vs. Net Lease
☐ Fed Ex, Airborne, UPS, etc.
☐ Quality of Office Build-out
☐ Comfortable Occupancy Date
☐ Signage Availability
☐ Availability of Space Planning
☐ Who pays for Space Planning
☐ Base Yr. vs. Expense Stop
☐ Smoking Policy
☐ On-site Leasing
☐ Availability of Day Maid

☐ Common Area Factor
☐ A/C & Heat Zoning
☐ Usable & Rentable Sq. Ft.
☐ Mail Delivery
☐ Quality & how often Janitorial
☐ Time to Build-out
☐ Reserved Parking
☐ Turnaround Time on signed Lease
☐ Building Operating Costs
☐ Annual Rental Increases
☐ On-site Management
☐ On-site Building Maintenance

This list may be useful as a checklist while touring office buildings during your search for office space.

Review this list and decide which items would be important to you in fulfilling your office space and personal or business needs. The items you choose will ultimately become your requirement.

CHAPTER 8

PRE-NEGOTIATION

THE FINAL OFFICE BUILDING TOUR CHECKLIST

LOCATION
☐ Close to Major Highways
☐ Close to Airport
☐ Close to Customers
☐ Close to Suppliers
☐ Close to my Home
☐ Close to Employees' Homes
☐ Close to Hotels
☐ Close to Restaurants
☐ Close to Shopping
☐ Suburban
☐ Downtown

BUILDING SITE ADVANTAGE
☐ High Visibility
☐ Easy Access (finding Property)
☐ Office Park
☐ Free-Standing
☐ Landmark Building

BUILDING'S INITIAL IMPRESSION
☐ Class A Building
☐ Class B Building
☐ Class C Building
☐ Well-Maintained Grounds

BUILDING'S CHARACTERISTICS
☐ Availability of Employee Parking
☐ Availability of Customer Parking
☐ High-Rise (Over 10 stories)
☐ Availability of Disabled Parking
☐ Mid-Rise (3-10 stories)
☐ Availability of Covered Parking
☐ Low-Rise (1-2 stories)
☐ Parking ratio 3 spaces per 1,000
☐ Over 200,000 sq. ft.
☐ Parking ratio 4 spaces per 1,000
☐ Over 100,000 sq. ft.
☐ Parking ratio 5 spaces per 1,000

☐ Over 50,000 sq. ft.
☐ Parking Convenient to Building
☐ Over 30,000 sq. ft.
☐ Condition of Parking Lot
☐ Over 10,000 sq. ft.
☐ Outer Appearance of Building
☐ Under 10,000 sq. ft.
☐ Cost of Parking (If any)
☐ Multi-Tenant Building
☐ Parking for Delivery Vehicles
☐ Single-Tenant Building

LOBBY & COMMON AREAS
☐ Atrium Lobby
☐ Standard Lobby
☐ Maintenance of Lobby
☐ Condition of Interior Landscape
☐ Condition of Floors
☐ Cleanliness of Bathrooms
☐ ADA Modifications in Place
☐ Condition of Elevators
☐ Response of Elevators
☐ Quality of Tenant Roster
☐ Building Security
☐ Coffee Shop
☐ Health Club
☐ Retail Shops in Building
☐ Building's Operating Hours _____ to _____

BUILDING AGE
☐ Currently Under Construction
☐ Newly Constructed (Under 1 Yr.)
☐ 5 Yrs. old or less
☐ 10 Yrs. old or less
☐ 15 Yrs. old or less
☐ 20 Yrs. old or less
☐ Rehab or Historical Building

Section I. Space Planning

You now have had a chance to review all the data you gathered on your building tours, and your selection has been narrowed to three buildings. You are about to request proposals from these three finalists. The proposal is an outline of the owner's proposed business terms. It is for your review, comparison, and ultimately the tool used for negotiating the business terms of your final lease.

It may seem odd that we are discussing the designing of your office space this early in the transaction, but it is usually at this point that the leasing agent will address the issue of space planning. It is being suggested now to give you a fair and accurate proposal, and to satisfy the owner's need to know approximately how much it's going to cost them to build-out your office space.

If the leasing agent suggests having a space plan done by his or her architect, there are some questions you must ask:

1.) "Who's responsible for paying the architect for the initial plan?"

In most cases, the landlord has an agreement for such plans with the architect. It's an expense that should be covered by the owner.

2.) "If the owner is paying, how many changes to the initial plan am I allowed before it starts costing me money."

Market tradition usually dictates how the landlord's architectural agreement is structured. I have found in some buildings and markets that you are allowed one or two changes at the owner's expense. Anything beyond this, you pay for.

3.) "If I decide to lease space in your building, are these charges going to be deducted from my tenant improvement allowance?"

Only the cost of additional drawings (such as your final working drawings), which will be submitted for permitting, should come off of your tenant improvement allowance. Watch this one carefully because the initial drawings might inadvertently be charged to you.

4.) "If I decide not to lease in your building, who pays for the space planning?"

Normally the cost is a risk absorbed by the building owner, but make sure.

5.) "What is your typical tenant improvement allowance?"

All buildings have budgeted a certain dollar amount to be set aside toward tenant improvement allowance per square foot.

6.) "Can I review the itemized costs?"

Most landlords don't like to do this but if pushed, most will allow you to review the itemized costs.

7.) "May I use an outside source for some of the items?"

Most landlords prefer to use their own contractor; it affords them better control of the overall construction project. Some will allow you to use outside sources as long as they have control over those sources and are protected by the appropriate insurance coverage by those sources.

8.) *"If I don't use my full tenant improvement allowance, can the remainder be held in escrow for future improvements?"*

If the entire tenant improvement allowance hasn't been used upon completion of your build-out, the landlord will usually hold the balance in his tenant improvement account until the end of the fiscal budget year. Unless this item has been negotiated as part of your lease, most likely your build-out is done.

9.) *"If I take the space 'as is' (no improvements), can I save money on my rent?"*

In some cases the landlord has made provisions for rent reductions of "as is" space in the building. Most landlords have not, but the question should be asked.

Remember that the initial space plan drawing is being done as a preliminary drawing from which the landlord can make a proposal offer to you. This will include an estimated build-out allowance. The proposal is a pre-lease document, which is usually non-binding on both parties. Its name—"proposal"— is just that. The landlord or tenant is proposing guidelines for the final lease transaction. A proposal is meant to be negotiated.

It's important to realize that before you make any further adjustments to the initial space plan, make sure you truly understand the items that are on the plan or must be added to the drawings. You should not agree to a final tenant improvement allowance amount until you are in full agreement with the final drawings and know the actual cost of construction.

Here are some important questions to ask the architect during your initial space plan meeting:

1.) What is a duplex plug?

2.) Location of the A/C and heating controls?

3.) A/C and heating zones?

4.) Type of lighting?

5.) What is a duplex circuit?

6.) Who pays for the telephone wiring?

7.) Who pays for computer connections?

The tenant should request copies of the existing blueprints to the space and of the demolition drawings for the proposed build-out. There are always ways to save some money in construction. Maybe you'll find a wall or sink that doesn't have to be moved.

BEWARE if the building's leasing agent asks if you have a space plan that they can work from; or he decides to draw the plan himself; or, he immediately sends you a proposal without pricing your potential construction. These are indications that the building ownership is frugal or in financial trouble, doesn't consider you a good risk, is about to give you a meaningless proposal, or they just don't know what they're doing.

Once you've met with the space planner and the building ownership has had a chance to estimate the cost of your construction, they may then ask for financial information on you and/or your company. Now that you have asked the owner to start investing his money on your transaction, he'll want to make sure there's a likely return on his overall investment.

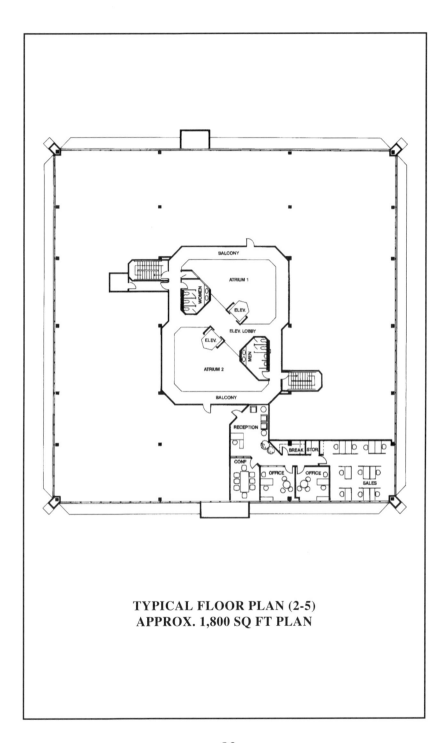

TYPICAL FLOOR PLAN (2-5)
APPROX. 1,800 SQ FT PLAN

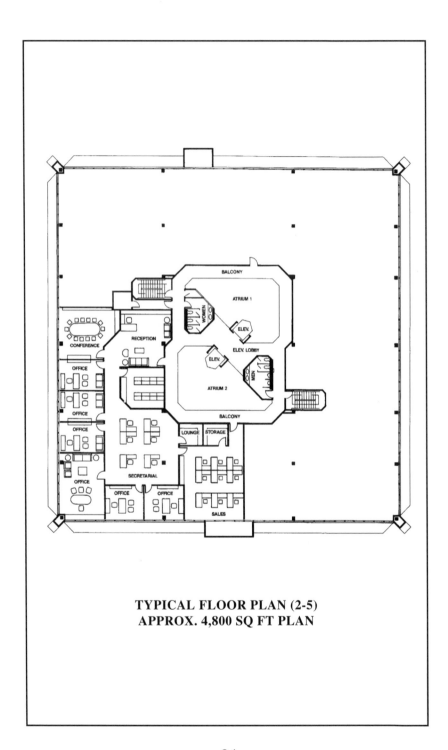

TYPICAL FLOOR PLAN (2-5)
APPROX. 4,800 SQ FT PLAN

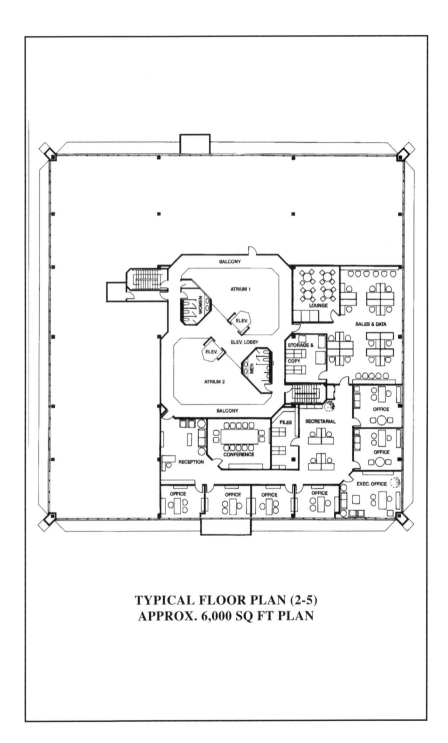

TYPICAL FLOOR PLAN (2-5)
APPROX. 6,000 SQ FT PLAN

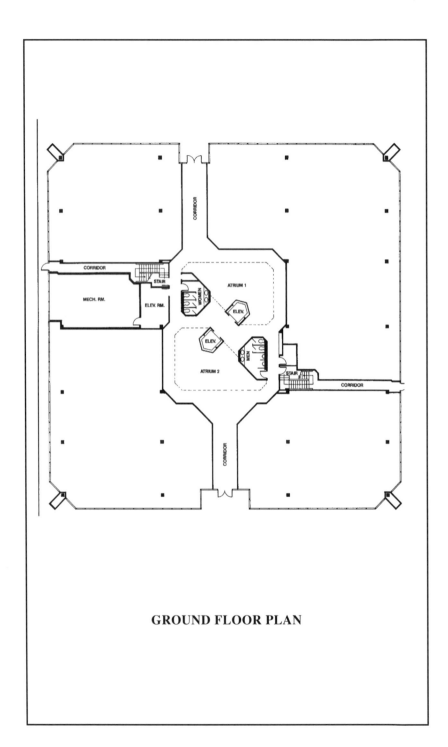

GROUND FLOOR PLAN

Section II. Supplying Financial Information

Now that you are about to spend some of the building's funds, this would be an appropriate time for the leasing agent to request financial data from you. If you are part of a well-known Fortune 500 company, he may not. But don't be insulted if you are asked to provide such information.

The request may be to see your company's annual report, profit and loss statements, balance sheets, bank and credit card references, or your tax returns. This is a common request and your immediate response will only help strengthen your negotiating position, unless your company is new or has weak financials. Your firm's financial strength, time in business, and credit history will help dictate how much risk the landlord is willing to take.

The proper information will assist him in structuring a proposal that will protect his interests, and offer you terms he feels will allow you to lease space in his building. Or, he will eliminate you as a prospect.

For some companies, financial information is considered a propriety. You may ask the landlord to sign a non-disturbance disclosure before handing over your financials. You should consult with an accountant to provide a sanitized version of your financial statement. These statements can be used to see what you've paid in the past, who you've done business with, and assess your financial risk to the prospective landlord.

Quite often, if the prospect hasn't been in business for a long period of time, or the landlord's inquiries into his financial references have not come back completely conclusive, the landlord may ask for the tenant to post a letter of credit toward the cost of constructing his space. A letter of credit is a letter guaranteeing payment up to a certain dollar amount from your bank or lender. If the landlord still feels he'd like to have you as a tenant, but he is unsure of your financial ability, he might ask for a personal guarantee.

A personal guarantee is risky. In case of a lease default, it puts you at risk personally. If such a default were to occur under a personal guarantee, you could lose your home, automobiles, vacation home and more. It is exactly as stated: a *personal* guarantee. You are held personally responsible for the payment and fulfillment of this debt.

Other types of guarantees would be the corporate guarantee or a guarantee offered by another related entity having stronger financials and the ability to cover the lease should you default.

Keep in mind that the landlord does have the right to request this information. The amount of information requested should be reasonable, and you can question any request that's made of you. It's important to understand that the landlord is about to invest quite a bit of money into the construction of your space. The more comfortable he is with you, the stronger your negotiating position in doing your deal.

CHAPTER 9

THE NEGOTIATION

Section I. Positioning

I'm sure most people would agree that it's best to negotiate when you have nothing to lose. You'll always get what you want and a little bit more.

In the early 1980s, I was working for a well-known national real estate brokerage firm. I was the leasing half of a two-man operation. The other gentleman in the office was one of the premier land brokers in Orlando. Together we were an incredible team, making a lot of deals and having a lot of fun.

With a newly fueled interest in the Orlando market, developers and buyers were flocking to the area in large numbers. Once they had bought the land to develop their new buildings, they needed someone to lease and manage these properties, so back they came. Some would give us the exclusive right to lease and manage their properties, and others made job offers. We always turned down the job offers, but gave them a list of good people to talk to. One developer was more persistent than the rest.

This gentleman was with a retail developer from Alabama. He told us he had been referred by a couple of gentlemen we had just sold some land to for a class A suburban office building. His company owned a piece of property in Melbourne, Florida, about 70 miles east of Orlando. He was here to find someone to lease and manage a multi-use project, hotel and office building they were planning to build on their site. He confided that his friends were very impressed with the way we handled their transaction, and specifically with my knowledge of the market. He further confided that his friends were about to make a substantial job offer to me and assured me that all he needed was some direction and introductions to strong leasing and management people in the Orlando market that might consider moving to Melbourne.

I set up the introductions for him with four people I felt would be interested in his offer. After completing his interviews he called and asked if I would join him for dinner as a thank you for the help and to discuss his impressions.

Over dinner that evening he indicated some interest in a couple of the people I had referred to him, but told me his real interest was in hiring me. I laughed and said I was quite happy right where I was. I was making good money and part of a great team. I had no interest in moving at all. He said, "Come on, I know it's going to cost me, but tell me what it will take." I restated my position of having no intention of leaving. I had too much going for me and just wasn't interested. Once again he said, "Look, I'll be back next week so just put down some numbers on paper for me. I don't care how ridiculous they may seem. Just let me take a shot at it." Finally I said, "OK, look. I'll put down something on paper for you, but remember there's no negotiating. Either you meet my conditions or drop the whole issue and move on, right?" He agreed.

Well, I put it down on paper. I did a little research and came up with an absolutely outrageous package. I asked for everything you can imagine plus a few more items. My base salary was triple what I was making, then I added bonuses, perks and even an ownership position in future properties. No way would anyone even consider this package. I was safe. He would look at it, laugh and leave.

The following week, he showed up, opened the envelope, looked it over, chuckled and said, "It's a start. We can negotiate this, right?" I said, "The deal is, accept those terms or move onto the next, remember?" He chuckled again and said, "I'll call you."

He called the next day. "Be at the executive airport tomorrow at 12:30. I'm flying down to pick you up, the boss wants to meet you."

The conversation on the flight to Alabama was centered around my unwillingness to negotiate. I reminded him repeatedly, "There is nothing to negotiate. I want to stay where I am." Finally he said, " If he agrees to meet your terms, you will accept, won't you?" "I told you I would, but that's the only way I'll move," I replied.

An hour-and-a-half later I was sitting in front of his boss. After the pleasantries and introductions, his boss said, "Let's talk about this package of yours. I'm willing to offer you..." I interrupted and said, "I've explained my position repeatedly. I hope you understand, I am very happy where I am. I don't want to make a move. You obviously won't meet my request, so I'll just leave now and go back to Orlando. I've enjoyed meeting you and thanks for your time." He looked at me and said, "I want you to start at the beginning of the month. Does that work for you?" "As long as you'll meet my terms and conditions," I answered.

I started at the beginning of the next month.

The point of this story is that I had nothing to lose and everything to gain. Had I wanted the job, I probably would have negotiated and had I negotiated, I would have lost.

Section II. Free Rent

This issue is so important that I felt I had to devote a whole section to it. Free rent is the single most damaging concession that can be made. It's like poison ivy. It is attractive at first, but once you've touched it, you're going to pay the consequences.

There was a time when free rent was exactly that. The landlord would give you a month or two rental abatement to simply close the deal and land you as a tenant. There was also a time when the landlord would base his rental rate on your usable office space, not knowing if he could charge for the building's common areas and remain competitive. Ah yes, those were the good old days.

In the 1980's, many markets in this country experienced a tremendous real estate boom. At least it appeared that way. Lenders had lots of money to lend on commercial real estate projects, and made it easily available to just about anyone wanting to build. All you needed was a reason, and a simple presentation to convince them how successful your project would be. To developers and would-be developers, easy money became as addictive as a drug. The more money you borrowed, the more you needed and more you got. New developers were popping up in record numbers. New buildings were popping up in both proven and unproven areas. Sadly, it was all happening at the same time. Over a three- to four-year period, millions of new offices sprang up overnight. In a blink of an eye, the amount of existing office space far exceeded demand. The result: *a total bust.*

This scenario created the ultimate tenant's market.

Tenants were at a premium. Developers and owners needed occupancy. They had promised these lenders full buildings at high rates, and they had to repay these loans. But how? Desperation set in.

Step one: find tenants. How? Offer them free rent. Get them in at any cost and when things get better in a couple of years, they'll pay the higher rate.

It starts with one building, one owner. A 5,000-square-foot prospective national tenant comes through the door. The owner has to make a deal so he offers the company six months free rent up front. In month seven the tenant will pay $16.50 a square foot, but it's got to be a five-year deal. In the owner's mind, if he gets this deal he has a credit-worthy tenant and he got the $16.50 rate he promised the lender. In reality, because of the free rent, the deal is worth $16.59 effectively for the life of the lease if he can get 5% annual increases. With six months free, the rate the tenant will pay in the fifth year of the lease will be $20.06 per square foot. The tenant will save $41,250 over the life of this lease.

The tenant visits the building next door and shares the offer that's just been made to him. The owner of the second building is in the same desperate position. He sees that the tenant is credit worthy so he offers him the first twelve months free rent at the same rate, but the term has got to be six years. Sounds good and your overall effective rate is $15.96 per square foot for the six-year life of this lease. Keep in mind you were originally willing to do a five-year deal—now you're committed to six years with a final annual lease rate of $21.06 per square foot. You'll save $82,500 over the initial five-year term. But since you've added an additional year (year six) at a rate that will probably be so far over-market at that time, you've actually spent an additional $22,800. Had you leased new space in year six or renegotiated a renewal at the end of year five, you would have been paying a fair market rate in the sixth year.

As you can see, if free rent is offered to you on the basis of no term extension, you'll save money over the term of your lease, based on the rate you are being quoted. Now the question becomes: "Was that quoted rate a realistic rate, given the condition of the market?" Remember—the developer got his loan based on a promise to the lender of getting a high rate. For that matter, so did the developer of the second building you visited. Well, $16.50 must be the market rate since it was quoted to you twice, right? It may be the market rate, but it's based on a false market. These rates were loan-driven, not market-driven. Only time can answer this question.

I will tell you though that ten years later those same buildings are no longer offering free rent. They're now more than 90% occupied and doing their deals at $15.50 per square foot. Five years ago those buildings were 80% occupied and doing their deals at $14 per square foot. If you took that six-year deal, with one year's free rent, in year six your rental rate would be $21.06 in a $14 market. Was it a good deal? How about the five-year deal with a fifth year rate of $20.06 in a $14 market?

Sometimes things are not what they appear to be. Concentrate on negotiating your rate, not free rent.

Section III. Building Operating Expenses

Here's something I want you to remember: Tenants *always* pay their proportionate share of the building's operating expenses.

The issue of operating expenses and its overages are the most overlooked and lightly touched upon aspect of the office building lease. When a prospective tenant is informed that his expense increases are based on 1996 or that his expense stop is $4.25, his usual response is, "What does that mean?"

94

It means you're about to find out the kind of building leasing agent you're dealing with. If they're straightforward, you'll get a clear picture of what to expect—with no surprises. If they're not, you'll hear about how wonderful and efficient their property is.

The tenant does have the right to request a full disclosure of the building's operating expenses. I highly recommend that you request and review these expenses before paying them.

The truth about operating expenses is that most buildings may call their leases "full service," but in reality the lease should be defined as a "modified gross lease."

In the case of a modified gross lease, let's look at the three scenarios presented below:

1.) Operating Increases based on Base Year 1996. If you signed your lease in 1996 you should not be billed for any overages in 1996. Let's say the building operated at $7 in 1996. This now becomes the dollar figure that all future operating expense pass-throughs will be based on.

In 1997 the building owner *anticipates* that the building will operate at $7.35 per square foot. The word "anticipates" is extremely important. Operating expense overages, unless otherwise agreed to in the lease, are typically billed and paid in advance. They are usually broken into monthly payments and added to your monthly rent. Some leases call for the following year's expense overages to be paid starting on January 1.

Other leases start them on your lease anniversary date. You're now probably asking, "How can they charge me for overages based on a fictitious figure?" Read your lease. They can, they do, and it's an accepted norm in the office building industry. With 1997's estimated building operating expense at $7.35, you will be billed an additional 35 cents per square foot throughout 1997.

At the end of 1997 the building owner compiles the actual figure of what it cost him to operate the building for the year. Let's say the actual 1997 operating expense was $7.50 per square foot. You will receive a bill for the difference between the 35 cents which you've been paying all year and the 50 cents which represents the real figure. So the landlord will bill you for the additional 15 cents per square foot. Conversely, if the real figure were to come to $7.15 per square foot, you should receive a credit of 20 cents per square foot.

This continues year after year until your lease expires—or should I say, until *after* your lease expires. That's right, if your lease expired in June, for instance, you would pay your anticipated operating expenses through June. At the end of the year, when the landlord has figured the actual operating expenses for that year, you're going to get a bill for the difference through June.

2.) Operating Expense Stops. An operating expense stop is a figure that is given in order to establish a base operating expense figure from which your increases will be added. Thus, the $7.50 figure representing 1996 expenses could be used as an expense stop. BEWARE: these are usually quoted at well below the actual operating expense cost of the building. For example, if an owner tells you that the first $4.50 is on him, and the building is operating at $7.50, that means the other $3 and everything added to it from then on, is on you. Other games that are played with these stops might be $4.50 on occupied space, and $1.90 on unoccupied. The owner has just hedged his bet on vacant space in the building. The higher the vacancy, the lower the $4.50 drops.

3.) Previous Year Used as the Base Year. If you were to move into the building in January, 1997, and you've agreed to a base year of 1996, you will most likely immediately be billed for 1997's anticipated operating expense overages. Don't be surprised. Remember that billing and payment is in advance based on the landlord's estimate.

At the beginning of this chapter, I stated that the tenant always pays their share of the building's operating expenses. Even though a gross lease is a lease that is all-inclusive, your rate will most likely be higher, to cover these costs. The full service (modified gross lease), as I've explained earlier, is a lease in which both the landlord and the tenant share in the payment of operating expenses. In a net lease, the tenant pays his own property taxes, insurance and janitorial costs. In a net net lease, the tenant pays his own property taxes, insurance, utilities and janitorial. In a triple net lease, the tenant pays the landlord the rent, and the tenant takes responsibility for paying all other related costs.

The following is a list of expenses eligible for increase under the tenant's pro rata share:
1.) Real estate taxes and assessments
2.) Gross rents, sales, use, business, corporation, franchise or other taxes, (except income taxes)
3.) Utilities not separately paid by the tenants of the building.
4.) Insurance premiums, including the cost of any self-insurance program which the landlord allocates to the building, and deductibles.
5.) Maintenance, repairs and replacement
6.) Refurbishing of common areas
7.) Cleaning, janitorial and other services
8.) Equipment, tools, materials and supplies
9.) Air-conditioning, heating and elevator service
10.) Property management costs
11.) Security fees
12.) Employees and contractors
13.) Resurfacing and restripping of walks, drives and parking areas

14.) Signs, directories and markers

15.) Landscape maintenance

16.) Rubbish removal

17.) Pest control

18.) Lighting fixture and bulb replacement

Operating costs should not include:

1.) Landlord's expense for legal services

2.) Income tax accounting

3.) Interest

4.) Depreciation

5.) General corporate overhead

6.) Capital improvements in excess of $_____, except to the extent that such capital improvements are necessitated by tenant's use or occupancy of the leased premises.

These inclusions and exceptions may vary slightly from market to market, but generally these lists are typically found in a building lease, based on a modified gross basis.

Section IV. "The Scorpion & the Turtle"

It was an unbearably hot day along the banks of the river. Not a cloud in the sky. The sun's rays seemed to be aimed directly on the turtle basking just three feet from the river's edge. He had been lying there for about half an hour and was giving serious consideration to crossing the river to find a cool shady spot.

"Hey turtle!" The turtle was startled. "Yeah you, turtle," said the voice. The turtle looked slowly to his left to see where this annoying interruption was coming from. And there it was. He was staring directly into the beady little eyes of a scorpion.

The scorpion continued. "Hot day huh? Hey look, I've got to get to the other side of the river and there's no way to cross. How about giving me a ride?"

The turtle looked at the scorpion and shook his head in disbelief. "You've got to be kidding," said the turtle. "If I give you a ride across the river, you'll sting me while we're crossing and I'll die. Leave me alone, find another ride."

"That's ridiculous," said the scorpion. "If I stung you while crossing the river, we would both drown. All I want to do is get across this river. You're my only hope. I promise—you are perfectly safe. I won't sting you, I don't want to die."

The turtle thought for a moment. The other side of the river was shady and cool and the scorpion made a good point. If he stung him, he'd be killing himself, too. Nobody could be that dumb. "OK scorpion, hop on my back. I'll give you a ride."

Halfway across the river the scorpion jumped on the turtle's neck, stung him and they both drowned.

Instinct vs. common sense. Instinct wins.

Section V. The Landlord

Who is "the landlord"? Or, who are you really dealing with?

In order to negotiate effectively, you must know who or what you're dealing with. In most cases, you're dealing with a system or an organization—not an individual.

The person showing you office space and negotiating with you is usually a leasing agent. Once the lease has been signed, the people you deal with are the property manager and the building staff. Their responsibilities are to lease and oversee the day-to-day operations of the property. And, achieve a profit for the building owner.

So far it sounds pretty simple, but the question still remains: "Who's the landlord?"

"The landlord" is the system that's been put in place to assure the profitability of the building owner's investment. A system is impersonal, uncaring, and exists for a single purpose: profit. This system can be operated by one or two people, or hundreds—depending on the size of the ownership entity and the number of properties owned or operated by the property owner.

You now know what motivates the building owner—profit. But what motivates the people who work for the owner? These are the people who you—the tenant—deal with. These are the people who make up the entity known as "the landlord."

The two most common types of motivation are "self-promotion" and "self-preservation."

"Self-promotion" is the achievement of personal or monetary gains. In the office building industry it can come in the form of a promotion, more authority, company recognition, or financial bonuses.

"Self-preservation" is the ability to survive; to keep a job and maintain income.

These motivations play a strong role in human nature and have become instinctive in all of us. For employees of the building owner, the only way to assure fulfillment of these instincts is to achieve the goal of the building owner:

profitability. The bigger the profit then the bigger their bonus, the stronger their corporate recognition, and the more secure their position.

It is vital to remember that as nice, knowledgeable and helpful as the building staff may seem, they are employed by the building owner—not you. Their job is to assure profitability for the building owner, thus they are instinctively motivated by self-promotion and self-preservation.

BEWARE OF THE SCORPION!

CHAPTER 10

THE LEASE PROPOSAL

Section I. A Typical Lease Proposal

The following is an example of a simple but typical lease proposal you might receive from a leasing agent:

117 BRADLEY POINT
PROPOSAL FOR THE CAPRI CORPORATION

December 8, 1985

AREA: Approximately 2,500 square feet of Rentable Area.

FLOOR: Twelfth (12th)

TERM: Five (5) years, commencing February 1, 1986.

RENTAL RATE:	Year	Base Rate (1)+	Expenses/Taxes (2)
	1	-0-	-0-
	2	16.00	5.69+/-
	3	16.00	5.69+/-
	4	16.00 (3)	5.69+/-
	5	16.00 (3)	5.69+/-

(1) Fixed rate and CPI adjustment annually as indicated for years 4 and 5.
(2) Actual Pro Rata Share of Operating Expenses and taxes to be paid by tenant as projected and adjusted to actual annually.
(3) 50% of CPI increase, first month as Base.

RENTAL CONCESSION	Landlord would waive Base Rent and Expenses/Taxes for the first twelve (12) months of the Lease Term.
OPTION TO RENEW	Landlord offers to Tenant the right to renew for two (2) years provided Landlord receives twelve (12) months prior written notice. Rental Rate for the renewal period would be at the then current market rate for similar space in the building.
TENANT IMPROVEMENTS OF ORIGINAL LEASED PREMISES	Landlord would provide a Tenant Improvement allowance of $16.00 per square foot of Rentable Area for construction of the Leased Premises.
OPTION TO EXPAND	Tenant shall have one (1) 1,000 square foot expansion option commencing the thirteenth month provided Landlord receives six (6) months written notice.
PARKING — MONTHLY	Tenant would have the use of two (2) parking spaces per 1,000 square feet of Rentable Area, on an unassigned and unreserved basis, in the building garage, at no additional charge to Tenant.
SERVICES	Landlord would provide electric power for general office use. Conditioned air would be provided Monday through Friday, 8 a.m.-9 p.m., and Saturdays from 9 a.m.- 4 p.m., national holidays excepted. Janitorial services would be provided five (5) days weekly.

| AFTER HOURS SERVICES | Additional non-standard hours of conditioned air are available at Landlord's then current hourly rates. |

The terms and conditions offered herein are available for your review and acceptance for fifteen (15) days, and would be incorporated in our Standard Lease Document. The Lease would be subject to the final approval of Walthrop, Inc., and its partners.

This example represents a standard office building proposal. Let's say this has been submitted to you for your review. It outlines the business terms of what the landlord hopes will be the business terms of the final lease. Don't get too excited about the terms and conditions being offered. Notice that the date of this proposal was 1986—not a good year for landlords.

To convert this proposal to a "letter of intent," the headline would be changed from "proposal for" to "letter of intent for." The final statement of terms and conditions would be a signature block for your acceptance. Letters of intent usually carry a disclaimer stating: "The terms and conditions of this Letter of Intent are not meant to bind the Landlord or the Tenant in any way." Although it may carry terminology stating that it is not meant to bind the parties, read it carefully.

The "letter of intent" format is usually used by landlords as a psychological tool. It is commonly felt in the commercial leasing business that once you—the prospective tenant—have signed a document such as this, you'll feel obligated, committed or more inclined to sign the final lease document. In short, they're getting you prepared for "the big one"—**the lease.**

Section II. Analyzing the Lease Proposal

Let's break down the lease proposal that you just saw in Section I.

1.) The building is a downtown property.

2.) You're being offered "approximately" 2,500 square feet of "rentable" space.   The reason for approximation is that until you've signed off as accepting the final construction documents/drawings, your square footage could vary. Also notice that the landlord is offering you a *rentable* amount of square footage. This means he is quoting you an amount of office space that includes the *common area factor* of the building. You will be paying rent on *rentable square feet*, not the *usable*, which is the amount of space found within the confines of your office space. Nowhere in this proposal does the landlord address the *common area factor* of the building. If you had asked this question during your tour of the property, you would know that it is 15%. If you deduct the 15% from the *rentable square footage*, you would know your *usable square footage* (the actual space you will occupy).

3.) The offer is based on a five-year lease term. You're scheduled to occupy this space beginning February 1, 1986.

4.) The "Rental Rate" is based on rentable square feet. On the surface it appears you're being offered a *flat rate*. But get out your calculator because that's not what you're being offered!

Year 1: You pay absolutely nothing. No rent, no expense overages, no taxes.
(Keep in mind that $5.69 under the heading "Expenses/Taxes" represents the expenses and taxes being paid to operate the building in 1985. It is also the amount you are agreeing to base

106

all operating expense and tax increases on. You will pay your proportionate share of any expenses or taxes that exceed this $5.69 figure.)

Year 2: Your "Rental Rate" is $16 per *rentable square foot.* This means that for the entire year you will pay $40,000 in rent plus (rarely is it minus) the difference between 1985's building expenses and taxes, and 1987's (which is Year 2 of your lease since you occupied in February 1986). Let's assume a 5% increase per year on expenses and taxes. Based on this assumption, the difference between 1987's operating expenses/taxes and 1985's would be approximately 58 cents per square foot. The building operates at $6.27 per square foot in 1987. Add $1,450 to the $40,000 for a total of $41,450 in Year 2. Your pro rata share is figured by multiplying your proportionate share of the building (percentage of building that you occupy) times the amount of operating expense/real estate taxes being paid by the building, over the $5.69 figure it was operating at in 1985.

Year 3: Your "Rental Rate" remains flat in Year 3 at $16 per *rentable square foot.* You will continue to pay $40,000 per year in rent. However, your operating expense/tax overage continues to increase by 5%, now giving you an overage of 90 cents per square foot. The building is now operating at $6.59 per square foot. This translates to an additional $2,250 per year to be added to your base rent of $40,000 for a total of $42,250 per year.

Year 4: If you've accepted this proposal, you've agreed to have your "Rental Rate" increase in Year 4 by one-half the annual CPI adjustment rate since February 1986. That's right— February 1, 1986. That's according to the terms stated in subparagraph #3 of the "Rental Rate" section. I'm sure you assumed your adjustment was to be based on one-half the CPI between 1988 (Year 3) and 1989 (Year 4)—but it wasn't caught during negotiations. This sentence should have been clarified and rewritten to reflect your understanding. It wasn't that your rental rate has gone from $16 per square foot based on annual 5% CPI increases divided by half, to $17.23 per *rentable square foot*, or $43,075.63 plus operating expense/tax overage of $1.23 per square foot or an additional $3,065.58 for a total of $46,141.21 per year.

Year 5: Your "Rental Rate"—assuming another annual 5% increase of CPI—increases an additional 2.5% to $17.66 per *rentable square foot* (or $44,152.52) plus operating expense/ tax overages of $1.58 per square foot (or an additional $3,940) for a total of $48, 092.52.

Added to this figure in many areas is state sales and use tax, or its equivalent. This could be an additional 5% to 10% depending on the state, county, or city where the building is located.

In analyzing the above proposed transaction, your total rental cost over the five-year term of the lease would be $167,228.15. This translates to an effective rate (average rate per square foot for the life of the lease) of $13.38 per square foot in rent. The one-year free rent dramatically lowered your average rent for the entire term. The operating expense/tax overage for the life of this lease was $10,705.58, which means your average annual operating expense/tax overage increase was 86 cents per square foot per year.

This is a very aggressive deal offered to you by the landlord of this particular building.

5.) Rental Concession. The landlord is offering you the first year of the lease at no cost to you at all.

6.) Option to Renew. You will have the right to renew this lease for a period of two years provided you inform the landlord in writing of your intention to renew. This must be received by the landlord a year in advance of your expiration date. In reality, it's a pretty generic offer since you haven't reserved a price.

7.) Tenant Improvements of the Original Leased Premises. The landlord is stating that he is willing to contribute up to $40,000 toward the build-out of your space. This amount usually indicates that the space has not been occupied before so the build-out will be started in an empty shell. It's important at this point to find out the owner's intentions. If the space is a shell, it may or may not already have the ceiling and A/C or heating in place. You have to find out if this $16 per square foot is being offered "below the ceiling." By asking this question you'll find out whether or not you're buying the A/C installation (including ducting, etc.) and the ceiling. If you are, start negotiating to get the offer "below the ceiling"—or as much of it as you can.

8.) Option to Expand. According to this proposal, you are being assured the right to expand provided you notify the landlord no later than six months prior to your thirteenth month of occupancy. In other words, if you're going to exercise this option you must notify them of your intention at the beginning of your seventh month of occupancy. The way this option is written, it does not guarantee that the space you'll be expanding into would be adjacent or connected to your existing space in any way.

9.) Parking—Monthly. The landlord is offering you two free parking spaces in his garage, for the life of the lease. The space is on a first-come, first-serve basis. Being a downtown building, it's common for parking to be paid for. The building's parking ratio is not addressed in this proposal, make sure you ask.

10.) Services. This is how the landlord defines his full-service offer, by explaining all that is to be included.

11.) After-Hours Service. If you have a tendency to work beyond the normal operating hours of the building, any services that you use (air-conditioning, heating, lights, etc.) will be billed at per hour of use at whatever rate you've agreed on with the landlord.

Summation: This offer is good for 15 days. Even though this offer is being made to you and the intention is to incorporate the above conditions in a standard lease, it hasn't been officially accepted by the landlord. His acceptance would come in the form of a fully executed lease by you and them. There are a few points that obviously have to be negotiated such as the CPI increase, clarification of the tenant improvement dollars, strengthening the renewal option, the option to expand, and the after-hours use clause. But the landlord seems to have sent a subtle message that these areas are open to discussion.

Compare Proposals. I said earlier that this proposal *appears* to be aggressive. However, we don't know exactly how aggressive it really is until we compare it to proposals from other competitive buildings. At this point, you always have one or two other buildings in reserve. Hopefully, you've requested proposals from the other buildings as well. Once you've analyzed all three proposals, it's time to make an apples-to-apples comparison.

Once you've broken down all three proposals then set them side by side and compare them item by item. You might find that the building you found most appealing will ultimately cost you an additional 50 or 75 cents per square foot over your second choice. Is your preference 50 to 75 cents per square foot better than the second building?

Now's the time to sit back and reanalyze your perfect scenario, your goal. Which building best fulfills your original vision? What do you have to do with each of these buildings and their proposals to make them fit your vision? Now re-rate them by setting up your first, second and third choices. Establish a game plan. Adjust these proposals until they meet your needs.

Once you're ready, call the leasing agent of the building you prefer, and set up an appointment to finalize the terms of the proposal. Using the market as your ally, let him know how much further he has to go to make the deal, and see how close he's able to come. At this point it's going to work or not work. If it works, tell him to prepare the lease for your review. If it doesn't work, move onto your second choice.

Section III. The Letter of Intent

The "letter of intent" is simply a lease proposal that requires the signature of the prospective tenant or both the prospective tenant and the landlord. It may or may not be a binding legal document depending on the terminology used at the end of the document.

Let's take a look at an example of a letter of intent:

LETTER OF INTENT

TO LEASE OFFICE SPACE

AT

LEXINGTON PLAZA

10/17/89

111

The following represents an outline of the basic business terms agreed to by Willow Broadcasting Corporation, D/B/A WXXX, and Severton Corporation. These terms form the basis from which a lease document will be completed for execution by both parties.

Tenant Name:	Willow Broadcasting Corp. D/B/A WXXX
Address:	149 W. Parker Avenue Lexington, MA 08757
Use:	Radio Station
Area:	5th floor = 2,500 usable square feet = 3,000 leasable square feet. Tenant will receive an elevator lobby entrance.
Base Rent:	$16.00 per leasable square foot.
Operating Expenses:	Tenant will be assessed its proportionate share of common area maintenance (CAM) including insurance, taxes and utilities.
Base Rent Abatement:	Six (6) months from rent commencement date
Cost of Living Adjustment :	None
Lease Term:	Five (5) years. There will be two (2) five-year options at a rate to be negotiated sixty (60) days prior to the expiration of the lease.
Rent Commencement Date:	Date to be mutually agreed upon.
Deposit:	First month's rent and security deposit equal to one month's rent.

Parking:	Landlord will allocate a total of sixteen (16) parking spaces to Tenant, free of charge.
Pylon Sign:	At no cost. Tenant shall receive signage on a pylon sign outside the building upon approval by the city of Lexington.
Build-out Allowance:	Landlord will provide Tenant with a total cash build-out allowance of $20.00 per usable square foot.
Space Planning Services:	An allowance of $.60 per usable square foot is provided by Landlord towards the professional services required to obtain a building permit from the city of Lexington. Millwork and other special details, interior design and furniture selection services are not included.
Press Release:	Tenant shall receive a local and national press release announcing its move to Lexington Plaza, to be paid for by Landlord.
Building Security:	Security will be provided 24 hours a day, 7 days a week.
After-Hours Use:	Tenant will be allowed access to the building 24 hours a day, seven days a week. Normal business hours are 7:00 a.m. to 6:00 p.m., Monday through Friday. Air-conditioning may be obtained on weekends and after hours with 24-hour notice to Landlord, at Tenant's expense.
Financial Statements:	Last annual statements and any subsequent interim statements must be delivered to Landlord prior to the execution of a proposed lease.

Based upon your review and acceptance of the above, the necessary Lease documents will be prepared for your final review and execution.

This letter is neither a contract nor an offer to lease and is intended to generally describe the principal terms presently acceptable to Severton Corporation. The proposed lease agreement is subject to the final approval of Severton Corporation and the Tenant, and in no event will there be any binding agreement until the final form of the lease has been approved by counsel for Severton Corporation, and the lease has been fully executed by both parties. Notwithstanding the foregoing, we will endeavor to maintain the principal terms described herein until November 17, 1989.

Accepted by:

SEVERTON CORPORATION   WILLOW BROADCASTING
                            CORPORATION. D/B/A WXXX

Signature_____   Signature_____

Print Name _____   Print Name_____

Title_____   Title _____

Date_____   Date _____

As you can see by reviewing the above letter of intent, it is simply a proposal with a signature block for your "psychological approval." The landlord feels that once he has you signing, it's a big step in your commitment to him, even though this particular example is a non-binding document.

Section IV. Analyzing the Letter of Intent

The terminology at the end of the "letter of intent" will dictate whether the agreement is binding or non-binding. In most cases it's used as a tool to get the prospective tenant "mentally committed" by signing a non-binding document. It is commonly felt that the letter of intent is a very strong "closing strategy."

Although the format is similar to the proposal, let's analyze this letter of intent in its entirety:

1.) The building is a suburban property.

2.) Your proposed use of the space is to run a radio station from this location.

3.) Your space will be located on the fifth floor of the building, and your usable square footage will be 2,500 square feet. Since the common area factor of the building is 20% (too high), your rent will be based on a leasable square footage of 3,000 square feet. The space will be located within direct view of the elevators.

4.) Your rate will begin at $16 per leasable square foot ($16 x 3,000 sq.ft.= annual rent).

5.) The operating expense clause tells you that the rental rate is being quoted on a net basis since you will be paying "your proportionate share of common area maintenance (CAM) including insurance, taxes and utilities." This indicates the operating expense rate per square foot will be added to the $16 rental rate. If the building is operating at $7 per square foot, you are actually paying $16 plus $7 = $23 per square foot.

6.) The landlord is giving you the first six months of the lease rent free. However, you will still be paying the operating expense portion of the lease.

7.) The $16 rate will remain constant throughout the term of the lease since there is no cost of living adjustment.

8.) The lease will have a term of five years and you will be allowed to renew for two additional five-year terms, but the rate will be negotiated at that time.

9.) The rent commencement date will be discussed and mutually agreed upon.

10.) The landlord is requiring that you pay a security deposit equal to your first month's rent and your first month's rent up front.

11.) You will be given sixteen parking spaces free of charge. Your parking ratio is 5.33 spaces per 1,000 square feet of leasable office space.

12.) The landlord agrees to put your company's name on an outside sign provided the city approves the landlord's installation of this sign.

13.) The landlord will contribute $20 per usable square foot toward the build-out of your office space. This is usable—not rentable. Therefore, you're being allotted $20 x 2,500 square feet, not $20 x 3,000 square feet.

14.) The landlord will pay 60 cents per square foot toward your final working drawings. This amount will not be deducted from your $20 tenant improvement allowance.

15.) The landlord, at his cost, will supply and send out a local and national press release announcing your leasing and occupancy in his building.

16.) The building will supply security in some form, 24 hours a day, seven days a week.

17.) You will always have access to your office space. However, if you require air-conditioning after allotted building hours, you must make those arrangements 24 hours in advance and must pay the landlord an additional charge for its use.

18.) The final paragraph states that you must supply the landlord with an annual financial statement and any other pertinent information for his approval before the lease is finalized.

This last paragraph indicates the strength of the letter of intent. If it is a disclaimer stating that you are about to sign a non-binding agreement, and the terms being offered to you are only good for thirty days, then it is non-binding. If it contains language that this agreement is binding on the tenant, or the landlord and tenant, you can rest assured you are signing a binding agreement.

Whether the format is a lease proposal or a letter of intent, it is important you understand that the negotiating has begun. These documents will ultimately outline the agreed-upon business terms between the landlord and tenant. Negotiate hard and ask for more than you want. You can be sure the landlord is. You will find that by pushing a little, you will usually uncover a few items in both the proposal and lease that the landlord has thrown in as giveaways. Some of them are easily identified because they're so outrageous. Others are very subtle. We'll discuss these in more detail when we analyze the lease.

CHAPTER 11

THE LEASE

Section I. If It's Not in The Lease, It Never Happened

It is vital that you remember: If it's not in the lease, it never happened! All that you have accomplished to this point means nothing if it is not stated in the lease or in one of the attached documents.

Before you invest any more of your valuable time or money, get a realistic understanding of how long it's going to take to turn around the lease. Once you've received the document, it should take you no more than seven to ten days—if everything's as it should be—to complete your review, your adjustments, and sign the lease. It is traditional that the tenant sign the lease document first.   It's important to find out how long it normally takes the landlord to review and sign the lease document. Remember, once you've signed the lease, you are now officially "on ice." By signing the lease, with your changes, you have committed to leasing space in this building, provided the landlord accepts your changes without any further adjustments. Unless you are looking for multiple locations, you can't sign another lease until this matter has been resolved.

Once you've signed the lease, time is no longer your friend. It is important that the issue of time be addressed throughout the entire leasing process. The question of how long each process takes should be asked starting from the time you first tour the building until you receive the fully executed lease document in your hand. The owner knows his lease document well enough to know the adjustments he can and cannot live with. Anything longer than a two-week turnaround, once you've signed the lease, is unacceptable. If the timing is vital to you, address it in the addendum of the lease by putting a time limit on the landlord.

When I first entered the commercial real estate business, I was told by my boss, "Don't be too concerned about all the garbage in there. What it comes down to is this: you pay me the rent on time and I won't bother you." Of course, that was in the 1970s. When we ran out of lease documents, we bopped down to the local stationery store and bought another package of them. The stationer had a file cabinet full of leases, all styles. You could buy a "landlord's lease," a "tenant's lease," an "easy lease," a "medium lease" or a "hard lease." You could buy them with automatic renewal options or without. They were about four pages long and printed on both sides. Times certainly have changed.

Today, there are as many different styles of leases as there are attorneys. Items in the lease change from building to building, company to company, city to city, state to state and even country to country. The only thing you can be sure of— unless you present the landlord with your own company-written lease—is that when the leasing agent presents you with a lease, you've just received a "landlord's lease." A lease that is meant to give the landlord every advantage throughout the term of the agreement.

At this point in the transaction, I **always** recommend that the prospective tenant have their attorney review the lease document. Remember—in most states, real estate law requires that leases be written by an attorney. This is a legally-binding document you must fully understand before you sign.

Once you receive the lease from the landlord, you should immediately review the business points of the lease and look for the obvious giveaways. The obvious giveaways in the lease are typically items that are so blatantly repulsive that your immediate response is, "They've got to be kidding. I can't live with that!" These have been put there to catch your attention, to get you to focus on items that the landlord never thought he'd get away with anyway. These are points that he intends to concede during negotiations. He'll list these as major concessions that he's already made to show how hard he's trying to make this deal work for you.

The real danger are the subtle giveaways. These are sometimes concessions the landlord would like to get if he can, but he'll back off these points if they're going to kill the deal. The subtle giveaway is much more difficult to find and sometimes in longer leases, the item is repeated more than once. The purpose of repeating the clause again in the lease gives the landlord the opportunity to concede the point in one paragraph, knowing he hasn't lost anything because you probably won't be looking for it the second or third time in another part of the lease.

Be sure that **everything** you've negotiated for—no matter how minute—is addressed somewhere in the lease document or the attached addendum. There is no such thing as a "side deal" or a "handshake" agreement with the leasing agent or property manager. If it's not included in the lease, it never happened. If the leasing agent has promised to upgrade the carpet, add a television, upgrade the electrical, allow you to store supplies in the adjacent space at no cost, or even allow your Cousin Wally to do the drywalling, make sure it's in there. By negotiating the business points, after receiving the proposal or letter of intent, you have already neutralized the important business items of this transaction. Just make sure they are stated to your satisfaction throughout the lease.

Now that you have reviewed the business terms of the lease, send it to your attorney for his or her review of the **legal terms**. It is important you stress to your attorney that his job is to address only the legal aspects of the lease. I'm sure you've heard real estate agents refer to attorneys as "deal breakers." The only time I've found this to be true is when an attorney oversteps his area of expertise by trying to give his client—the tenant—business advice, not legal advice. Your attorney's responsibility is to soften and neutralize some of the legal issues that would put you at a disadvantage during your tenancy in the building. It is his job to convert this lease from a "landlord's lease" to a document that is mutually beneficial for both the landlord and tenant, so that it can be quickly signed and accepted by you and the landlord.

Once this is done, make an appointment with the building owner or leasing agent to finalize the terms of the lease. Review your changes with him or her, explaining the reason for each. Once you've gotten to the point where everything appears to be acceptable, go ahead and sign the lease. Be sure to initial all changes.

It is customary for the prospective tenant to sign the document first. If you are dealing directly with the owner, or signing authority, you can complete the transaction right there. More than likely, you'll be dealing with an agent for the owner. If this is the case, keep in mind that he or she can only give you an indication of what is probably acceptable to the owner. This individual does not have the authority to sign; therefore, they can only guide you. Once the owner has signed the lease, the deal is done and the negotiating is over. Whatever is in the lease is part of the transaction. If it is not in the lease, it never happened and it probably never will happen.

A word of caution! Before you sign the lease, be sure the lease and the appropriate attachments have been finalized.

Review everything thoroughly before signing and be sure that your final space plan with all your changes is correct, that you've been given a firm and final price of construction, and that it's reflected in the construction work letter.

Section II. Terms Commonly Found in the Office Lease

The following information will give you a better understanding of some commonly used terms as well as how they are applied and some of the potential dangers involved when used in a standard office lease.

ACCESS—Tenant will allow landlord access to their suite.

Beware: The only time the landlord should be allowed free access to your space is in case of an emergency or to provide janitorial services. Other unsupervised access to the tenant's space should be pre-arranged with the tenant. The landlord should give the tenant at least a twenty-four hour notice, preferably in writing.

ACCORD & SATISFACTION—A statement used to protect the landlord in case of dispute. Allows the landlord to accept funds or other compensation from the tenant without effecting the landlord's position in the dispute.

Beware: Have your attorney review this paragraph. This item is usually determined by existing law. In many states, if a landlord accepts funds during a dispute that's been initiated by the landlord, the acceptance of funds is an indication the dispute has been settled. In such states consider this a potential "giveaway paragraph."

ALTERATIONS BY TENANT—A statement limiting the conditions under which a tenant may make alterations to their leased space.

Beware: Avoid terminology such as "landlord's sole discretion." Adjust this to say "reasonable" or "At the discretion of both landlord and tenant."

Most likely this paragraph will require the tenant to restore the premises to its original condition, prior to the work being done, supply the landlord with drawings or plans of your proposed alteration and have him sign off on what items must be removed at lease expiration.

AMENDMENT; WAIVER; APPROVAL; CONSENT— Conditions governing exceptions or changes to the original lease document. It usually restricts such changes or approvals to be given in writing.

APPLICABLE LAW—Statement that the lease shall be construed according to the laws of the state, province or local jurisdiction.

ASSIGNMENT & SUBLETTING—A statement in the lease controlling the assignment or subletting of space. It will also state whether you can or cannot sublet or assign the space.

Beware: Initially this paragraph is written strongly in favor of the landlord. Adjust language such as "sole discretion of landlord" to read "reasonable discretion." Avoid "recapture clauses" if you can. These give the landlord the right to take back the space or terminate your lease in case of a sublease.

The landlord may require that the subtenant be of equal or greater financial strength as the current tenant thus requiring financial approval of your subtenant. Avoid this if you can.

The landlord's major concern is that he is receiving his rent on time and the business that is occupying the space is not a detriment to the building.]

ATTORNEY FEES—A clause commonly found in leases declaring—that in case of a legal dispute—which party is required to pay attorney fees.

Beware: This is an item governed by local law, unless waived by the acceptance of such a clause. It's most likely a giveaway and should be adjusted to read "prevailing party should be entitled to their reasonable attorney's fees, paid for by the losing party."

AUTHORITY—A clause stating that the company about to enter into the lease is doing business legally in the appropriate state, and that the person(s) signing the lease have the authority to do so.

Note: This simply assures the landlord that he or she is doing business with an entity that is legal and that the individual(s) signing this document have the right to do so.

BINDING EFFECT; GENDER—Statement in the lease indicating the lease shall be binding upon not only the current parties to the lease but also their successors and assigns. Lease terminology is using the words "landlord" and "tenant" uniformly throughout the lease regardless of gender or number or fact of incorporation.

Beware: This clause states that the lease cannot be terminated by either party in case of a death.

BROKER INDEMNIFICATION—A statement declaring the use or non-use of a real estate broker in the transaction. If one has been used, this paragraph should state who it is.

Note: The purpose of this paragraph is to indicate whether or not a broker has represented the tenant, and to identify the broker. If the tenant has not used a broker, it will avoid an unknown broker showing up after lease execution, demanding a commission.

BUILDING SERVICES—This is an important statement in the lease, indicating what you as the tenant can expect to be supplied for services as part of this lease. It indicates whether this lease is intended to be full-service/gross lease or net/triple net. Usually in this paragraph the landlord also states that if he cannot provide a service for a specified amount of time, you cannot withhold rent.

Beware: Most landlords will not agree to allowing you to withhold rent, but give it a shot. Try to negotiate the right to withhold rent if the landlord is unable to provide certain services.

CAPTIONS & SECTION NUMBER—Indicates that captions and section numbers throughout the lease; using the words "landlord" and "tenant"; and, verbs and pronouns in the singular number are used uniformly throughout the lease regardless of gender, number or fact of incorporation of parties to the lease.

CASUALTY—A declaration in the lease of what happens in case of a natural disaster.

Beware: Rent should be abated in the event that the building is deemed uninhabitable. This clause also should be adjusted to reflect that the landlord or the tenant have the right to terminate the lease if reconstruction of the building or of the tenant's space takes longer than three months.

CONDEMNATION—A declaration in the lease of what happens if part or all of the building is condemned.

Beware: Rent should be abated in case of building condemnation. This clause should be adjusted to reflect that the landlord or the tenant have the right to terminate the lease if said condition is not remedied within three months. Do not allow the landlord to take away your right to sue the authorities condemning the property for damages resulting from your loss of personal property, fixtures and other items you've paid for.

CONSTRUCTION CONDITIONS—This states the terms and conditions governing the build-out of the tenant's space.

CROSS-DEFAULT—If the tenant has more than one lease in the building and defaults on one lease, the tenant thus defaults on all leases within the building.

Beware: If at all possible avoid any kind of "cross-default clause" by negotiating a position where each space stands on its own.

EFFECT OF BANKRUPTCY—Terms and conditions of how this lease will be handled by both parties in case either one enters bankruptcy.

Beware: Bankruptcy laws govern the treatment of creditors, so the landlord should not have the right to terminate.

ENCUMBERANCE—Statement that the tenant will not be able to encumber, mortgage or pledge this lease in any way unless first approved by the landlord. Simply a protection of landlord's position regarding the lease.

ESTOPPEL CERTIFICATE—A certificate verifying that the lease is in full force. Usually states the terms and conditions governing the current status of the tenant's business relationship with the building. Typically used by the landlord if he or she wishes to refinance or sell the property.

Beware: It is extremely important that the information on this document is accurate, before signing. By signing you are verifying that the information is correct and you could be held responsible for complying with this information at a later date. For example, if the square footage is wrong, you could be charged for additional space.

EVENTS OF DEFAULT—A list of ways this lease would be considered in default.

Beware: Make sure all the items listed are specific and allow you reasonable time to cure such defaults. Typically ten days for rent and thirty days for other cures are considered appropriate.

Issues governing the landlord's default may also be covered in this paragraph. Be sure you are notified by the landlord in writing of the landlord's ability or inability to cure these defaults. And, give yourself the right to cure the default, sue because of the default, or terminate the lease resulting from the default.

EXECUTION—The signing of the lease.

FORCE MAJEURE—Acts of God.

Beware: Tenant's rent obviously should be abated during any period in which the premises are deemed totally unusable. If the building or the tenant's space cannot be made usable within a certain period of time (usually 90 to 120 days), the tenant should have the right to terminate the lease.

HAZARDOUS SUBSTANCES—Dictates the policy of payment for removal and states who takes responsibility for the existence, payment, and removal of such substances.

Beware: If the tenant is not the cause of the problem, he or she should not be responsible to pay for the correction or removal of the problem.

HOLD-OVER TENANCY—This section dictates the building's policy on a tenant remaining in their space beyond the term of the lease without an agreement. It also states the penalties to be enforced in case of a hold-over tenancy. Sometimes 150% to 200% of rent agreed upon under the terms of the original lease.

Beware: During the initial lease negotiations, you may try to negotiate an additional thirty or sixty days of occupancy at a specified rate in case a future space is not ready in a timely manner. Your goal is to avoid or delay the additional 50% to 100% increase as best you can. The purpose, from the owner's perspective, is that if you are not going to stay, he or she wants you motivated to move as quickly as possible in order to release your space.

INABILITY TO PERFORM—Defines inability to perform on behalf of both landlord and tenant, and penalties resulting from such inability.

Beware: (See "Events of Default")

INSURANCE; INDEMNITY—This paragraph defines the amounts and types of insurance both parties will be required to have, or not have.

Beware: You should be required to carry public liability and property damage insurance of not less than $250,000, or combined insurances of $1 million. The landlord should carry coverage insuring the building in the event of fire and other major disasters. The landlord's insurance should also include a loss of income and utility interruption coverage. This means the landlord would be reimbursed for loss of rental in case of such an event.

LANDLORD'S LIEN—Watch out for this one! This clause gives the landlord the right to an express contract lien on, and security interest in, all personal property, fixtures, furnishings or merchandise in the leased premises together with any insurance and other proceeds of the tenant. Under this clause the landlord may also have the right to remove any and all items from the space and to store them at the tenant's expense. He can also sell or dispose of this property at his sole discretion. Proceeds from such a sale would be applied first to the cost of the sale, secondly to cover costs of storage and/or removal, and finally to pay any damages, attorney's fees, costs or other sums of money due from the tenant to the landlord.

Beware: This is one of those blatant giveaways! If he or she won't back off this clause, you don't need to be in their building.

LANDLORD'S RESERVED RIGHTS—This clause simply states that the landlord has the right to sell the land, the building, change the name or address of the building, change rules and regulations, etc. And, the tenant's lease would remain in force and would remain substantially unchanged.

Beware: Insist on a "non-disturbance clause" if one is not already in the lease. This clause should assure you that in the case of a sale or foreclosure of the building, your rights as a tenant would continue. And, the new landlord or owner will assume all responsibilities toward your tenancy in the building.

LIENS—For the purpose of the lease, the tenant does not have the right to subject or jeopardize the building, the landlord, or any other interest of the landlord's.

LIMITATION OF THE LANDLORD'S LIABILITY— This clause limits the tenant's ability to pursue damages. If the tenant decides to sue for damages, he or she is limited to look solely to the landlord's interest only in this property.

Note: This states how notices will be delivered and to which address for both parties, Landlord and Tenant.

OCCUPANCY; LEASE COMMENCEMENT DATE— This paragraph defines occupancy and lease commencement. They are not always the same. If a tenant were given a period of free rent, occupancy would be defined as the day the tenant occupied the space. Lease commencement would begin the day the tenant starting paying rent. This clause also states the rights of the tenant if space is not delivered in a timely manner.

PARKING—Tells how many parking spaces the tenant will be allotted. Lease should also indicate whether spaces are reserved or unreserved, paid or free, covered or uncovered, etc.

Beware: If you're negotiating for free parking, make sure the lease states that you will not be charged for parking; how many spaces will be allocated; and, where they will be located (i.e. on- or off-site).

RECORDING/MEMORANDUM OF LEASE—This paragraph states the lease is a legal document and at any time, at the landlord's sole discretion, the document can be recorded and placed on public record.

RELATIONSHIP OF PARTIES—Statement that the landlord and tenant are not in business together and are not partners.

RELOCATION—The landlord has the right to relocate the tenant—usually within the building or property—at anytime during the life of this lease. It is usually governed by certain conditions.

Beware: In the case of a large tenant situation, try to eliminate this clause. If you cannot, make sure the lease states that all expenses (moving, computer relocation, stationery changes, etc.) are covered. Try to stipulate that the new space must be considered comparable by both landlord and tenant.

REMEDIES—This is a list of things the landlord may do if the tenant defaults on the lease.

Beware: Make sure this list is specific and you have enough time to remedy any defaults.

RENT—Money to be paid to the landlord by the tenant in return for occupying space in the landlord's building. It is usually paid on a monthly basis and stated in terms of annual rent and monthly rent.

Beware: Make sure the dollar amount on the lease agrees with the amount you negotiated.

REPAIRS—This clause will sometimes list examples of the type of repairs the landlord will make. It also will indicate who is responsible for payment of repairs. Items could be hidden within this clause so check it carefully.

Beware: Make sure you state that any repairs to be done by the landlord will cause minimal disturbance to your business. Negotiate some alternatives if the landlord does not, or is unable to, make the necessary repairs in a timely manner.

RULES & REGULATIONS—A schedule of the building's rules and regulations attached to the lease. They simply regulate actions the landlord deems appropriate behavior by you, your employees and your guests while in his building.

Beware: Read these rules and regulations carefully. They sometimes eliminate the use of small appliances such as coffee pots, microwave ovens, etc. You may need to negotiate or at least be aware of these exclusions.

SCHEDULES & EXHIBITS—Lists any changes to the lease being referred to in an attached document.

SECURITY DEPOSIT—This simply reflects the amount of money requested by the landlord and paid by the tenant to be held in escrow. It insures the landlord against damage to the office space while you are in tenancy. If there are damages, the money can be used to make the appropriate repairs.

Beware: This clause should state how deductions will be determined and give a time limit for the return of the security deposit.

SEVERABILITY—If any term or clause in this lease is proven to be invalid, it will have no effect on the remainder of the lease, and the lease will remain in force. This clause, however, will usually state that if such a clause were to effect the agreed-upon income that the landlord is to receive from the tenant's space, then the landlord would have the right to cancel the lease.

SIGNS—Indicates the type of signage the tenant will be allowed during his tenancy. If outside signage has been negotiated, it will appear here, along with the terms governing that type of signage. Door signage and tenant roster signage will also be addressed in this clause, as well as who pays for the signage.

SUBORDINATION—This lease would be considered subordinate to any loans or liens placed on the building.

Beware: Add a non-disturbance clause to assure that in case of foreclosure the lender will continue to honor your lease and accept all obligations of the landlord.

SUCCESSORS & ASSIGNS—The terms and conditions of this agreement would remain in force and unchanged even if the lease were assigned or taken over by the tenant's heirs.

Beware: This clause states that if the lease were to be assigned or taken over by another party, that party would be obligated to live up to the terms and conditions of the lease and death does not terminate the lease.

SURRENDER OF PREMISES—Tenant agrees to surrender the leased property in good condition at the end of the lease term.

Beware: Make sure you have stipulated in the lease that the landlord will perform a final walk-through of the space with you once you have vacated. Also make sure you're not held responsible for normal wear and tear of the premises.

TENANT'S PROPERTY—This clause defines items that are property of the tenant and states that if such property is left behind after tenancy, the landlord has the right to move it at the tenant's expense.

Beware: Generally, items that are attached are considered the landlord's property, whether they were paid for by the tenant or the landlord. It is best to inventory such property with the landlord prior to taking possession of the space to avoid confusion once you vacate.

TENDER & DELIVERY OF LEASE—Reminder that the lease will become effective after it is fully executed by both the tenant and the landlord.

TERMS & DEFINITIONS—This section holds the key to the applied definition of business terms used in the lease. Terms such as "base rent," "square footage," "operating costs," "common area," "broker of record," "lease commencement date," "lease expiration date," "term of lease," "lease year," "permitted use," "suite number," "security deposit," "tenant's pro rata share of building," etc.

Beware: Verify this entire section for accuracy. Remember—what is in the lease is what you have to live with.

TIME—Statement that "time is of the essence."

USES—This defines what type of business will be conducted in the leased space.

Beware: Keep this clause as generic as possible. If you find it necessary to sublease the space, you won't want to be restricted by this "use clause."

UTILITIES—Landlord states that the utilities being supplied to the tenant are according to the terms and conditions of this lease.

WAIVER OF SUBROGATION—Landlord and tenant hold each other harmless if their insurance companies cover a particular claim.

Beware: Make sure that agreeing to a waiver of claims against the landlord does not invalidate your business interruption insurance coverage—if you have such coverage.

WAIVER OF TRIAL BY JURY—Both parties would be willing to waive a trial by jury in case of a dispute arising out of the lease.

Beware: A clause like this is usually a giveaway—**eliminate it!**

These definitions are here to simplify their meaning and to guide and inform you when used in the context of a lease document. These are certainly not definitions you would necessarily find in your dictionary.

Section III. Typical Attachments to a Lease:

Schedule 1 – Rules and Regulations

Exhibit "A" – Leased Premises (a drawing designating the location of your space on a particular floor, or wing of the building.)

Exhibit "B" – Floor Plan/ Improvements (the final working drawing of your space. This should be the space planner's drawing complete with all improvements, that you will approve.)

Exhibit "C" – Work Letter and Construction Budget (a complete written description of every item the landlord will be paying for under your tenant improvement allowance.)

Addendum to Lease – Any additions or changes to the lease should be found on this document. The changes on the addendum will take precedence over the item it affects on the lease. This is usually attached to a lease as an add-on to the original lease negotiations.

Amendment to Lease – This is a document reflecting any changes to the lease document after the original document has been signed. It is an after-the-fact type of document. It can be typically used for any changes to the lease or can be used in lieu of writing a new lease for a renewal or expansion of space.

CHAPTER 12

CHANGES, ADDITIONS & ATTACHMENTS
TO THE LEASE

Section I. The Addendum to the Lease

An addendum to the lease is an attached document that is an addition to the original lease document. Its purpose is to add, adjust or change the intent or meaning of a statement within the lease itself. An addendum is done in conjunction with the original lease and is usually signed by both the landlord and tenant, as part of the lease.

The addendum, unless stated differently in the agreement, will supersede or override the paragraph or clause in the lease that addresses the same issue.

Here is an example of an addendum to the lease:

ADDENDUM TO LEASE

THIS ADDENDUM TO LEASE ("The Addendum") is entered into this 14th day of December, 1994, between Grisham Corporation, a Florida Corporation and Williams & Penski, P.A. A Florida Professional Association, for lease of 1,000 square feet at Whitmore Centre, Medford, Florida.

RECITALS

A. On December 14, 1994, Landlord and Tenant entered into a lease agreement ("the lease") with respect to certain leased premises (described therein as "leased premises"). This addendum, when executed by both parties shall become binding on the parties and the Addendum and the Lease Agreement shall collectively be referred to as the "Lease". All terms, covenants and conditions contained in this

Addendum shall have the same meaning as the Lease and shall govern should a conflict exist with the previous terms and conditions.

B. Landlord and Tenant desire to modify the terms, covenants and conditions of the lease as hereinafter set forth.

NOW, THEREFORE in consideration of the premises and other good and valuable consideration in hand, paid by the parties hereto, the receipt and sufficiency of which is hereby acknowledged the parties agree as follows:

1. Paragraph 1.25 of lease shall be changed as follows: 1.25 "Parking Spaces," shall mean four (4) non reserved parking spaces during the term of the Lease.

2. Paragraph 4.1 is hereby amended to provide that the Tenant's Base Rent shall be abated for a period of six (6) months from the Commencement Date, provided however, that the abatement is Base Rent shall not be considered for purposes of computing adjustments to rent as set forth in Paragraph 4.2.

3. So long as the Tenant is not in default under the terms and conditions of the Lease, Tenant shall have a First Right of Refusal to lease the additional 1,000 square feet of space contiguous to suite 500. This First Right of Refusal expires on June 14, 1995, or if Landlord has a bona fide third party offer, acceptable to the Landlord, to lease all or part of the remaining space on the fifth floor. Landlord shall give the Tenant the opportunity to lease up to 1,000 additional square feet on the fifth floor prior to accepting the third party offer. Tenant shall have ten (10) days after Landlord gives Tenant notice of the bona fide third party offer to exercise its right of first refusal for the space. If Tenant does not exercise its first right of refusal and Landlord rents a portion of the fifth floor to a third party or if Tenant exercises its first right of refusal for less than 1,000 square feet, tenant shall still have a right of refusal for the remaining portion of the additional 1,000 square feet, within the six (6) month period from the Commencement Date in accordance with the terms of this paragraph.

Signed in the Presence of: LANDLORD:
Grisham Corporation.,
a Florida Corporation

By:_____
as its President

TENANT:
Williams & Penski,
a Florida Professional Association

By:_____
as its

138

Section II. The Final Floor Plan

Review this document very, very carefully. This is your office space. Everything you want or need in your office must be on this plan. The blueprints, which will be submitted for governmental permitting, will be drawn from this final space plan. Your firm and final cost for construction will be based on the items in this drawing. And, ultimately, the space you will be occupying and paying rent for during the next three to five years is based on this drawing.

You will be asked to review and approve this plan by signing or initialing somewhere on the same page. Once you've signed it you have acknowledged that indeed these plans are exactly what you want and you fully understand the cost of achieving it. Make sure everything you have agreed to is there. If it isn't, *you* **will be held responsible,** *not* **the landlord!**

I have include an example of a final floor plan on the next page.

Section III. The Construction Work Letter

You'll usually find the building's "construction work letter" attached to the lease as an exhibit. The work letter specifies the quality and quantity of materials to be used in your office space build-out. It also usually indicates the dollar amount the landlord will contribute in tenant improvement allowance towards your build-out.

If used properly, this letter should explain what the landlord considers a typical tenant build-out. It should also point out that the tenant improvement allowance being allotted to your office space is intended to cover the cost—or a portion of the cost—of only the items designated in the work letter as building

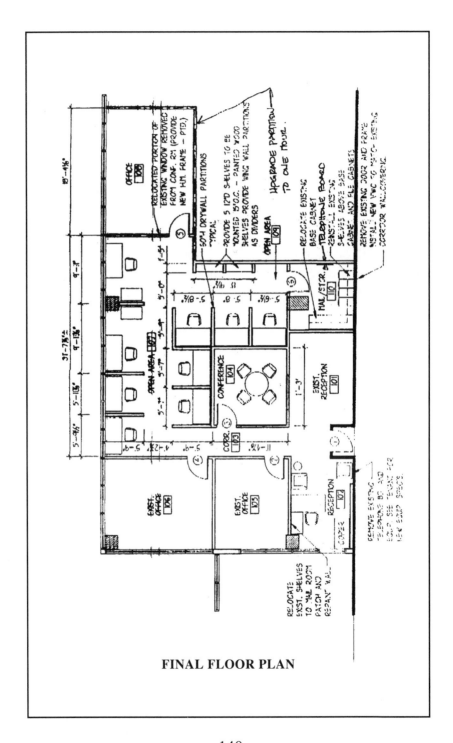

FINAL FLOOR PLAN

standard. The purpose of the work letter is to inform you that the landlord will deliver a basic, no-frills space and not cover the cost of upgrades such as sinks, cabinetry, shelving, carpeting, electrical, A/C, etc.

If you are able to upgrade some of these items as part of your lease negotiations, or if the landlord is willing to cover the cost of the upgrades under the tenant improvement allowance, you must either change the work letter, item by item, to reflect these agreed-upon changes, or write the appropriate clause in the lease addendum.

Often the landlord has given you the impression, after pricing your initial space plan, that he feels he can cover your build-out cost with the tenant improvement allowance he is offering you. His initial pricing is a "ballpark guess" at best. Never sign a lease and never sign off on the construction work letter until the final drawings are completed, approved by you, and you are given a final and firm price of how much it is going to cost to build-out your office space the way you want it.

Once you have signed the final drawings indicating your complete approval, they then are attached to and become part of your lease. Once you sign the construction work letter, you've agreed to the items to be supplied in the build-out of your office space. This, too, is part of your lease and you'll have to live with it.

Once you've been given the firm and final price, have the landlord also sign off on your plans and include a statement regarding items that may have been inadvertently missed by the landlord in pricing the build-out. Make him responsible for covering the cost of such items. You will find the landlord is covering himself by stating that if the tenant makes changes or additions to the plans, the tenant will pay. Your statement should read that if the landlord has inadvertently missed items in the final pricing of construction, the landlord should pay.

I recently had a landlord forget to include the cost of carpeting and baseboard in the final price of construction—a $14,000 error! His response to the tenant: "I didn't forget the carpeting. You created the overage with your upgrades. Read the work letter." In reviewing the tenant's paperwork documenting the entire transaction, it was obvious where the mistake was. Because the work letter had not been negotiated, we had to find other areas to reduce the $14,000 overage.

Read *and negotiate* the construction work letter.

Here is an example of a typical construction work letter:

THE CONSTRUCTION

WORK LETTER

Tenant: Whiz Bang Productions

Suite No: 4324

1. Plans and Specifications

By, January 30, 1994, Tenant shall furnish to Landlord layout plans and specifications approved by Tenant, and in sufficient detail to permit Landlord to design all of the work covered thereby. Landlord shall cause its Architects and Engineers to prepare architectural, mechanical and electrical plans for the leased premises on the basis of Tenant's approved layout plans and specifications. Landlord shall submit such plans and specifications to tenant who shall have five (5) business days to approve such plans in writing. The cost of two (2) sets of preliminary plans and one (1) set of final plans of the Landlord's work in Paragraph 3 shall be borne by Landlord, and Tenant shall bear the cost of any other plans or design services. Where applicable, Tenant shall select paint colors, carpet and other materials so as not to delay progress of work.

2. Conduct of Work and Pricing.

Landlord shall promptly submit the approved plans and specifications to its contractor, and shall thereupon instruct its contractor to proceed with Landlord's work as outlined in Paragraph 3 below. Any changes thereafter made by Tenant which changes Landlord's work shall be considered changes persuant to Paragraph 4 below. Landlord shall promptly notify Tenant of the costs to be borne by Tenant and Tenant shall have three (3) business days within which to approve such costs. Tenant shall pay to Landlord those improvement costs to be borne by Tenant before Landlord will commence to finish out of the leased area.

3. Landlord's Work.

Landlord agrees to have its contractor install, up to $10.00 per square foot, the following improvements in the leased premises:

1) TENANT INTERIOR PARTITIONS - 1/2" gypsum board both sides of 3-5/8" metal studs at 24" on center with vinyl wall base both sides of wall and two coats of flat latex water-based paint both sides of wall. The amount of demising wall partitioning is to be equally divided between two adjoining tenants.

2) DEMISING WALL PARTITIONS - 1/2" type "X" gypsum board both sides of 3-5/8" metal studs with 3-1/2" batt insulation in wall cavity. Partitions are carried to the metal deck, requiring the ceiling grid to be cut and patched back against the wall. Vinyl wall base is included on both sides of partitions plus one coat of flat latex water-based paint both sides of partition.

3) ENTRY DOORS - 3'0" x 8' 0" x 1-3/4" mineral core flush doors with veneer faces in hollow metal frames. Both sides of door are stained, with frame painted and caulked.

4) TENANT INTERIOR DOORS - 3'0" x 7'0" x 1-3/4" wood door with solid core with metal frame, stained with standard hardware.

5) ELECTRICAL (DUPLEXES) - One (1) duplex wall receptacle per each 100 square feet of rentable space.

6) TELEPHONE (OUTLETS) - One (1) telephone wall outlet per each 150 square feet of rentable area.

7) SIGNAGE - One (1) tenant identification sign to be provided by Landlord and installed in accordance with Landlord's standards.

8) CEILING ASSEMBLY - 2'0" x 4'0" acoustical panels with metal grid.

9) MECHANICAL - All mechanical work, which means standard office requirements, will be provided by Landlord. Any additional mechanical work deemed by Landlord to be over standard (i.e. self contained AC units for computer or sound rooms, extra heat pumps for specific areas) shall be borne by the Tenant.

10) LIGHTING - 2'0" x 4'0" recessed fluorescent lighting allowance = one (1) fixture per each 80 square feet of rentable area.

11) WATER FIRE PROTECTION SYSTEM - All water fire protection work including the main trunk lines and connecting pipes in the Tenant areas and the installation of the sprinkler branch lines and heads will be provided by Landlord in accordance with required codes. The cost to relocate or add heads to comply with the approved space plan shall be borne by the Tenant.

12) FLOORING - 26 oz. (Minimum) carpet will be provided in all Tenant areas (Includes base molding).

13) WINDOW COVERING - Standard 1" mini-blinds in all exterior windows.

4. Changes

If Tenant, after approving the final plans and specifications, shall request any changes to such plans and specifications, then Tenant shall be responsible for any costs incurred with respect to revising such plans, and shall further be responsible for additional improvement costs incurred as a result of such changes. Landlord shall advise Tenant of the estimated costs and time delay resulting from such changes prior to performing any work thereon. Any delay in completing the leased premises caused by such changes or prospective changes shall not in any manner affect the Lease Commencement Date or the Tenant's liability for the payment of rent from such commencement date, and under such circumstances, Landlord agrees to make the leased premises ready for Tenant's occupancy not later than the Lease Commencement Date plus the number of days delay resulting from Tenant's said changes or prospective changes.

5. Tenant's Special Requirements.

Any delay in completing the Leased Premises caused by any special or custom equipment, materials or finishes specified by Tenant shall not in any manner defer the Lease Commencement Date nor Tenant's liability for the payment of Rent from the Lease Commencement Date, and under such circumstances Landlord agrees to make the Leased Premises ready for Tenant's occupancy not later than the Lease from such special or custom equipment, materials or finishes.

The above provisions are agreed to.

DATE:_____

LANDLORD:
AWARD DEVELOPMENT CORPORATION

By:_____

TENANT:

_____

144

Section IV. The Versatility
of the Lease Amendment

The *lease amendment* and the *lease addendum* are very closely related. They both adjust, eliminate, or add to the original lease document. The major difference between the two is that the *addendum* is executed in conjunction with the lease. It is usually done and executed at the same time as the lease to directly and immediately effect certain terms of the lease. The *amendment* is a document that is added to the lease at a later date. It may be added to correct something that was missed in the original lease document or in the addendum. Or, it can be used for renewals, expansions, changing suite numbers or suites, assignment of lease, and any other change occurring within the lease to be accomplished at a date after the signing of the lease.

The lease amendment must be executed by both parties in order to become part of the lease. In cases such as lease renewal, expansion or even in the case of tenant relocation, the amendment is being used in lieu of a new lease. On such occasions I would strongly recommend that you, the tenant, take this opportunity to negotiate a stronger position for yourself. Or, possibly negotiate to correct item(s) you're not pleased with in your original lease.

The following story is an example of opportunities that can be created through the use of a lease amendment. Recently a client of mine was informed by his landlord that he must relocate to make room for an expansion of one of his neighbors. My client was very unhappy about this proposed relocation so he looked at his lease and read the "relocation clause." Sure enough, the landlord had the right to relocate him. The clause did, however, state that the space he was to be relocated to would have to be considered "comparable" to both the landlord and the tenant. It couldn't exceed or reduce his current square footage by more than 10%, and the landlord would pay all of the tenant's expenses incurred by such a relocation.

The landlord proposed several spaces as alternatives to my client—none of which were comparable. The dimensions of the proposed spaces did not allow my client to duplicate or even come close to duplicating his current floor plan, which worked perfectly for his business.

The landlord was losing patience. He had just signed an agreement with my client's neighbor, allowing them to expand into his space. The agreement stipulated that if the expanding tenant wasn't able to occupy this particular space by a certain date, due to the landlord's inability to deliver the space, the rent on all the space they occupied, which was sizeable, would be reduced by $3 per square foot for the remaining four years of their lease.

My client received his first unkind letter from the property manager: "We consider all the space we've shown you comparable, pick one or else. You are not living up to the terms and conditions of your lease." (The language wasn't quite this strong, but that's basically what they were saying).

"What do I do?" asked my client, "I really like the building. I love my space, none of the spaces they've offered me work and now they're going to throw me out." "Not necessarily," I said. "Is there any space in this building that might work for you?" "Sure, there's some space in the corner of the third floor," he told me. "It's a little more space than I need and I really can't afford to pay more for space than I am paying now. I've seen it, they haven't offered it to me, but it would work." I told my client, "This is a perfect opportunity to negotiate. Comparable can mean more than just physically comparable. We'll write a proposal on the third-floor space and tell the landlord what he has to do to make the space comparable."

The proposal was written, my client offered a rental structure equal to what he was currently paying, and asked for several other items including a television set for his newly acquired second conference room. He came out about $10,000 ahead and moved to the third floor. The landlord was able to expand his neighbor in a timely fashion. It was a win-win situation for everyone.

This entire transaction—the relocation of my client, the appropriate adjustments to his original lease, the expansion of his neighbor and their adjustments—was handled by lease amendment.

Here is an example of a lease amendment:

AMENDMENT NUMBER 3

THIS AMENDMENT TO LEASE (the "Amendment") is entered into this 1st day of April, 1992, by and between Crown Title Company whose address is 2030 Center Street, New York, New York, 10014 ("Tenant") and Sterling Development Corporation, 2100 Main Street, Melbourne, Florida 32801 ("Landlord").

RECITALS

A. On December 1, 1990, Landlord and tenant entered into a lease agreement ("the Lease") with respect to certain leased premises, precisely called ("the leased premises"). This amendment when executed by both parties shall become binding on the parties and the amendment and the lease agreement together with any addenda or previous amendments shall collectively be referred to as the "lease". All terms covenants and conditions contained in this Amendment Number 3 to lease shall have the same meaning as in the lease, and shall govern should a conflict exist with previous terms and conditions.

B. Landlord and tenant desire to modify the terms, covenants and conditions of the lease as hereinafter set forth.

NOW THEREFORE, in consideration of the premises and other good and valuable consideration in hand, paid by the parties hereto, the receipt and sufficiency of which is hereby acknowledged, the parties agree as follows:

1. Recitals. The parties hereto agree that the recitals (the "Recitals") are true and correct and the Recitals and the Lease referred to therein are incorporated and made a part of this Amendment to Lease.

2. Amendment. The Lease is amended as follows:

A) Amend Paragraph 1B of Lease, Paragraph 2a of Amendment number one, and Paragraph 2a of Amendment number two, to reflect a change in "Base Rent" of:

	Annual Rent	Monthly Rent
Year one	$14,000.00	$1,166.67
Year two	$14,560.00	$1,213.33
Year three	$15,142.40	$1,261.87

B) Amend Paragraph 2A of lease, "Lease Renewal Commencement" to begin May 1, 1992. Also amend in Paragraph 2A of lease, "Lease Expiration Date" to reflect an new expiration of April 30, 1995.

C) Delete Paragraph 3C.

D) Amend Schedule "C" of Lease "Tenant Work Letter" to reflect that Landlord will contribute $9.00 per rentable square foot towards the improvement of tenant's leased space.

3. Remaining Terms and Conditions. Except as modified hereby, the remaining terms, covenants and conditions of the lease shall remain unchanged and in full force and effect.

4. Effective Date. This Amendment shall be effective and binding upon both parties upon signing, unless otherwise scheduled herein.

IN WITNESS WHEREOF, Landlord and Tenant have executed and delivered this Amendment to Lease under seal on the day and year first written above.

WITNESSES: LANDLORD
                                    STERLING DEVELOPMENT CORP.

_____   By:_____

_____   Name:_____

                                    Title:_____

                                    Date:_____

WITNESSES: TENANT
                                    CROWN TITLE COMPANY, INC.

_____   By_____

_____   Name:_____

                                    Title: _____

                                    Date _____

Where Tenant is a corporation, the above signed warrants that he/she is an officer of the corporation and is duly authorized to execute this Amendment to Lease on behalf of the Tenant. Landlord may require a certified corporate resolution attesting to that fact.

This Amendment to Lease shall be effective only when it is signed by both the Landlord and the Tenant.

Once there is an existing lease document, an amendment can be used to make any changes to the lease. It can be used to correct errors in the original lease, change dates or rental amounts, adjust clauses and even reconstruct the lease during future negotiations and transactions. By using this document only the items specifically addressed in the amendment will change or supersede those clauses meant to be changed in the lease.

Renewals, subleases and assignments are just a few issues that can be addressed in an amendment, saving you the trouble of having to renegotiate the entire lease.

CHAPTER 13

THE TENANT BUILD-OUT

Section I. Estimating the Cost of Construction

"How much does it really cost to move a wall?" "I need just one more room, it can't be that expensive." "I could go out and buy that same door for $50. How come you're charging so much?" These are all questions that come up once the prospective tenant finds out how much it costs to build-out their office space. It's an area that creates a great deal of anxiety and tenant mistrust.

So, to help you out, here is an itemized breakdown of costs, as submitted by a general contractor, to renovate an existing office suite of approximately 2,000 square feet.

XYZ CONSTRUCTION COMPANY
ESTIMATE SUMMARY SHEET

SUMMARY TOTALS:

LABOR:	$3,612	LABOR BURDEN	$1,373	LABOR M/U	0.00%
MATERIAL	$2,502	SALES TAX:	$163	MATERIAL M/U	0.00%
SUBS:	$8,155	NET CUT & ADD	$0	SUBS M/U	0.00%
EQUIPMNT	$0	BOND:	$0	EQUIPMNT M/U	0.00%
EXPENSE	$0	TOTAL MARKUP:	$2,371	EXPENSE M/U	0.00%
				GENERAL M/U	15.00%
		TOTAL PRICE:	$18,175		

MARKUP DATA

LABOR RATE:	38.00%
M/U ON LAB BURDEN:	0.00%
SALES TAX RATE:	6.50%
M/U ON SALES TAX:	0.00%
BONDED (Y/N/2):	N

Includes: Every Line

Description	Labor	Material	Subs	Equipment	Expense	Burden	Labor Tax	Sales Markup	+Add	-Cut Total	Job%	Div #
Div 1 General Conditions	1442	1200	182				548		78	517	3967	21.8%
Div 2 Sitework & Demolition	720	0	0				274		0	149	1143	6.3%
Div 6 Carpentry	142	38	100				54		2	50	387	2.1%
Div 8 Door,Windows&Glass	180	0	0				68		0	37	286	1.6%
Div 9 Finishes	379	611	3668				144		40	726	5568	30.6%
Div 15 Mechanical Construction	0	0	1520				0		0	228	1748	9.6%
Div 16 Electrical Construction	0	0	1521				0		0	228	1749	9.6%
Div 17 Renovation Extras	749	653	1164				285		42	434	3328	18.3%
Totals for Above	3612	2502	8155			0	1373		163	2371	18175	100.0%
Plus Bond, if Req'd											0	0.0%
Grand Total:											18175	100.0%

The above is a breakdown of the overall construction of the office space. Now let's take a look at the costs, item by item.

ESTIMATE DETAIL SHEETS

Cost Code	Description	Quantity AL	GP	Labor /unit	Total	Other /unit	Tp	Supplier	Total Notes	Wrksheet
DIV 1 - General Conditions										
1.211	PROJECT MANAGER	3 WKS		100	300	0	M		0	
1.215	SUPERINTENDENT	3 WKS		300	900	0	M		0	
1.330	LAYOUT	6 HRS		15	90	0	M		0	
1.371	TELEPHONE	0.75 MO		0	0	150	M		113	
1.711	DAILY CLEAN-UP	1516 SF		0.1	152	0	M		0	
1.731	DUMPSTER FEES	2 LD		0	0	250	M		500	
1.740	FINAL CLEANING	1516 SF		0	0	0.12	S		182	
1.780	WARRANTY WORK	1LS		0	0	100	M		100	
1.810	SMALL TOOLS/MISC.	1LS		0	0	25	M		25	
1.872	PICK-UP	0.75 MO		0	0	250	M		188	
1.878	VEHICHLE MAINTENANCE	1LS		0	0	50	M		50	
1.879	FUEL	3 WKS		0	0	75	M		225	

TOTAL LABOR=1442   TOTAL OTHER=1382   MARKUP=517

LABOR BURDEN=548   SALES TAX=78   CUT/ADD=0

TOTAL=3967

153

Sort By: Cost Code   Est #:

Cost Code	Description	Quantity	AL	GP	Labor /unit	Labor Total	Other /unit	Tp	Supplier	Total	Notes	Wrksheet

DIV 2 - Sitework and Demolition

Code	Description	Quantity	AL	GP	/unit	Total	/unit	Tp	Supplier	Total	Notes	Wrksheet
2.060	DEMOLITION	16 HRS			45	720	0	M			0	

TOTAL LABOR=720   TOTAL OTHER=0   MARKUP=149
LABOR BURDEN=274   SALES TAX=0   CUT/ADD=0
TOTAL=1143

DIV 6 - Carpentry

Code	Description	Quantity	AL	GP	/unit	Total	/unit	Tp	Supplier	Total	Notes	Wrksheet
6.320	WOOD BLOCKING	35BF			0.75	26	0.5	M			18	
6.825	RELOCATE EXISTING CABINET	4HRS			24	96	25	S			100	
6.826	MILLWORK	0LS			0	0	0	S			0	
6.832	PHONE BOARD	1 EA			20	20	20	M			20	

TOTAL LABOR=42   TOTAL OTHER=138   MARKUP=50
LABOR BURDEN=54   SALES TAX=2   CUT/ADD=0
TOTAL=387

DIV 8 - Doors, Windows and Glass

Code	Description	Quantity	AL	GP	/unit	Total	/unit	Tp	Supplier	Total	Notes	Wrksheet
8.151	INSTALL INTERIOR DOOR	4 EA			45	180	0	M			0	
8.444	INTERIOR GLASS WINDOWS	0 LS			0	0	0	S			0	

TOTAL LABOR=180   TOTAL OTHER=0   MARKUP=37
LABOR BURDEN=68   SALES TAX=2   CUT/ADD=0
TOTAL=286

Includes: Every Line
Sort By: Cost Code
Est #:

Cost Code	Description	Quantity AL	GP	Labor /unit	Total	Other /unit	Tp	Supplier	Total	Notes	Wrksheet

DIV 9 - Finishes

Cost Code	Description	Quantity AL	GP	/unit	Total	/unit	Tp	Supplier	Total	Notes
9.261	INTERIOR PARTITIONS	30LF		0	0	17.05	S		512	
9.264	FULL DEMISING WALL	35LF		0	0	28.17	S		986	
9.266	MISC. DRYWALL PATCHING	1LSF		0	0	200	M		200	
9.268	KNEE WALLS	6LF		0	0	15.5	S		93	
9.270	FURNISH CEILING TILE	579SF		0	0	0.275	M		159	
9.271	INSTALL CEILING TILE	667SF		0.11	73	0	M		0	
9.272	REWORK CEILING GRID	140LF		1.8	252	1.8	M		252	
9.274	STOCK DRYWALL	54BDS		1	54	0	S		0	
9.330	CARPET	90 SY		0	0	12.5	S		1125	
9.333	VINYL BASE	240LF		0	0	0.85	S		204	
9.952	FINISH DOORS/FRAMES	3EA		0	0	35	S		105	
9.954	PAINT WALLS 2 COATS LATEX	2680SF		0	0	0.24	S		643	
9.955	PAINT SHELVING	0LF		0	0	0	S		0	

TOTAL LABOR=379
LABOR BURDEN=144

TOTAL OTHER=4279
SALES TAX=40

MARKUP=726
CUT/ADD=0
TOTAL=5568

DIV 15 - Mechanical Construction

Cost Code	Description	Quantity AL	GP	/unit	Total	/unit	Tp	Supplier	Total	Notes
15.510	RELOCATE SPRINKLER HEADS	4 EA		0	0	95	S		380	
15.511	ADD SPRINKLER HEADS	1 EA		0	0	110	S		110	
15.610	RELOCATE S/A GRILLS	2 EA		0	0	30	S		60	
15.611	ADD S/A GRILLS	2 EA		0	0	80	S		160	
15.612	RELOCATE R/A GRILLS	2 EA		0	0	15	S		30	
15.613	ADD R/A GRILLS	2 EA		0	0	30	S		60	

155

Sort By: Cost Code   Est #:

Cost Code	Description	Quantity AL	GP	Labor /unit	Total	Other /unit	Total	Tp	Supplier	Total Notes	Wrksheet
DIV 15 - Mechanical Construction (Cont)											
15.614	RELOCATE SLOT DIFFUSER	3 EA		0	0	40	0	S		120	
15.615	RELOCATE T STATS	2 EA		0	0	60	0	S		120	
15.617	FIRE DAMPERS	2 EA		0	0	120	0	S		240	
15.618	TRANSFER DAMPERS	2 EA		0	0	120	0	S		240	

TOTAL LABOR=0   TOTAL OTHER=1520   MARKUP=228
LABOR BURDEN=0   SALES TAX=0   CUT/ADD=0
TOTAL=1748

Cost Code	Description	Quantity AL	GP	Labor /unit	Total	Other /unit	Total	Tp	Supplier	Total Notes	Wrksheet
DIV 16 - Electrical Construction											
16.110	SINGLE POLE SWITCH	3EA		0	0	33	0	S		99	
16.112	DUPLEX RECEPTACLE	9EA		0	0	33	0	S		297	
16.115	PHONE STUB/UPS	18EA		0	0	16	0	S		288	
16.117	NEW CIRCUIT HOME RUNS	90LF		0	0	1.8	0	S		162	
16.120	RELOCATE LIGHT FIXTURES	13EA		0	0	20	0	S		260	
16.122	EMERGENCY BALLASTS	1EA		0	0	165	0	S		165	
16.124	EXIT LIGHTS	1EA		0	0	125	0	S		125	
16.125	ELECTRIC DEMO	1LS		0	0	125	0	S		125	

TOTAL LABOR=0   TOTAL OTHER=1521   MARKUP=228
LABOR BURDEN=0   SALES TAX=0   CUT/ADD=0
TOTAL=1749

Sort By: Cost Code   Est #:

Cost Code	Description	Quantity AL	GP	Labor /unit	Total	Other /unit	Tp	Supplier	Total Notes	Wrksheet
DIV 17 - Renovation Extras										
17.001	WOOD BLOCKING	35BF		0.75	26	0.5	M		18	
17.002	RELOCATE SHELVING	4HRS		24	96	10	M		40	
17.003	REINFORCE PONY WALLS	3 EA		75	225	75	M		225	
17.004	REMOVE ENTRY DOOR IN ML RM	1 EA		65	65	0	M		0	
17.005	RELOCATE RECESSED ENTRY	1 LS		125	125	50	M		50	
17.006	RELOCATE CONFERENCE RM DR	1 LS		75	75	0	M		0	
17.007	FULL DEMISING WALL	4 LF		0	0	28.17	S		113	
17.008	MISC. DRYWALL PATCHING	1 LS		0	0	200	M		200	
17.009	CLOSE DOORWAYS	2 EA		50	100	25	M		50	
17.010	KNEE WALLS	12 EA		0	0	15.5	S		186	
17.011	FURNISH CEILING TILE	258 SF		0	0	0.275	S		71	
17.012	INSTALL CEILING TILE	333 SF		0.11	37	0	M		0	
17.013	CARPET	20 YDS		0	0	12.5	S		250	
17.014	CARPET PATCH & ENTRY	1 LS		0	0	100	S		100	
17.015	WALLCOVERING IN CORRIDOR	1 LS		0	0	125	S		125	
17.016	SINGLE POLE SWITCH	1 EA		0	0	33	S		33	
17.017	DUPLEX RECEPTACLE	3 EA		0	0	33	S		99	
17.018	PHONE STUB/UPS	6 EA		0	0	16	S		96	
17.019	PHONE CONDUIT HOME RUN	30 LF		0	0	1.25	S		38	
17.029	ELECTRIC DEMO	1 LS		0	0	1.25	S		125	

TOTAL LABOR=749   TOTAL OTHER=1818   MARKUP=434
LABOR BURDEN=285   SALES TAX=42   CUT/ADD=0
                                                 TOTAL=3328

This is the construction cost breakdown that the landlord or the building's leasing agent usually sees once you've undergone your initial space planning. By reviewing this, you should have a better understanding of construction costs, on an item-by-item basis.

I strongly suggest you ask the building leasing agent to supply you with the itemized cost breakdown, and the right to shop price on some of the items to be included in your space. There may be items you requested the contractor to include in your build-out that you could find at lower prices. While recently having his new office space built out, a client of mine purchased his own wooden entry doors with glass inserts for $1,200/installed, and a dishwasher for $600/installed. The contractor's prices were $3,000 for the entry door and $1,000 for the dishwasher. Price-conscious tenants can avoid tenant improvement overages and unpleasant surprises.

Maintain your own construction file throughout the planning and build-out of your space. Stay on top of the process from initial space planning throughout the build-out. If you have thoroughly thought out your needs and carefully reviewed the final drawings, making sure everything you need will be supplied, there should be no need for changes and therefore no need for construction overages and unpleasant surprises.

Section II. The Build-Out

Believe it or not, the construction of your new office began back when you requested a proposal. If you recall, in Chapter 10 ("The Lease Proposal"), when you first requested a proposal from the building leasing agent, you were asked to supply some information on your financial status, then a space plan was drawn for your new space.

Your proposal request was the initial indication to the leasing agent that you were seriously interested in his or her building. It was also a request for the landlord to start risking some money to secure you as a tenant. The financial information you supplied helped the landlord decide if you were worth the gamble he was about to take.

The typical arrangement between the landlord and an architect for initial space-planning services can range between 10 cents per square foot to 30 cents per square foot—depending on the market location of the building. The arrangement usually allows for the tenant to be space planned one time, and allows a couple of changes to that initial plan. The larger your requirement, the larger the landlord's gamble. For instance, if you chose another building after allowing them to draw up your space plan, the landlord would still have to pay for the architect's services.

Now here's the tricky part. Once you have signed a lease and have agreed to be a tenant in the building, this expense is now yours unless the lease states it is the landlord's expense. Read the work letter attached to the lease. This attachment will itemize everything to be included in your build-out. It will also list the items being paid for through the "tenant build-out allowance" allotted by the landlord. Remember—architectural services are part of the cost of construction.

You should also keep in mind, in order for the construction of your space to begin, the construction company will first need a building permit from the city, county or other local governmental authorities. This means additional architectural documents and drawings at additional expense. These additional drawings must include a final set of plans, which will reflect your electrical needs, any adjustment to plumbing, sprinkler heads, A/C and heat ducting, as well as movement of walls, doors, etc.

You will be asked to sign off on these final drawings, and a copy will become part of your lease. The final plan that you have signed is the plan that will be used to build-out your space. Remember, it's now part of the lease. If you've missed something in the final plan, it won't be built unless you're willing to sign a change order and pay additional dollars for the change.

The final plans (usually two or more) will be submitted to the local government for their approval. This approval will be given in the form of a permit to build your space. Once the permit is received and posted in your space, construction is ready to begin.

The work letter also indicates how changes will be handled, how the plans will be handled and how additional charges will be paid. It will state the amount allotted you for tenant improvement allowance—usually in terms of "the landlord will pay up to" a certain amount. The work letter will list the building standard materials; how they will be treated in a typical build-out; and, it will address any special requirements the tenant may have and how these requirements will be handled.

While your space is under construction, visit with the building property manager and check on the progress of the space to make certain everything is correct, on time, and running according to the budget you anticipated.

This is the time when a tenant's first unpleasant surprise may crop up. You may have been led to believe the amount allotted in tenant improvement allowance was "more than enough" to cover all costs of your build-out. Once again, if it's not written that way in the lease, the addendum or the work letter, you're gambling. If you, as the tenant, want to be sure your construction costs are covered, have it written in the lease, the addendum, or the work letter, that the landlord will pay for all construction costs.

Quite often, the leasing agent's initial intentions are good, but the tenant improvement allowance quoted to you was done at the proposal stage of the transaction. The dollar amount was based on your first set of space plans. By the time your final drawings are complete, you've had the opportunity to make changes to the original plan. Prices change when the plans change. The final price won't be known until the final drawings are completed and these drawings are priced for construction.

This is why it's so important for you to have a firm and final price on the construction of your space before you sign the lease and before you sign those final drawings!

I've seen it happen so many times. An item is missed in the plans only to be added during the actual construction of your space—at your expense. Sometimes the item is big. It could be carpeting, electrical or air-conditioning,; something costing thousands of dollars and because you missed it, you just blew your budget. Notice I said *you* missed it. It is highly unlikely the property manager will admit to the mistake. He or she will refer to the work letter and will tell you they won't cover the upgrades that caused the expense. They are protecting the owner's profit and they are motivated by self-preservation.

To avoid such mistakes, you may want to consider hiring an interior designer, negotiating their fees into your deal. Even if the landlord won't cover the designer's cost, it's worth a few extra dollars to have a professional on your side to review the final drawings and to ensure it doesn't cost you unplanned thousands.

The construction stage is probably your first opportunity to work closely with the individual who is overseeing the day-to-

161

day operations of the property: the property manager. This is the person you'll be dealing with for the next three to five years. The individual who can make your tenancy a pleasure—or a nightmare! If during your negotiations, the building leasing agent considers the management of the property an amenity, the property manager should be introduced to you and involved in your initial space planning.

If the property manager has not been included at the space-planning stage, ask that they be included. It will give you an opportunity to meet and determine if this person is capable. By doing this, you're assured of a smooth transition from the signing of your lease, through the build-out of your space, on into your occupancy. After all, this is the person who has to deliver on the leasing agent's promises. When the transition is handled this way, there's less chance of unpleasant surprises.

CHAPTER 14

MOVING INTO YOUR NEW OFFICE SPACE

Section I. When in Doubt, Call an Expert

So far I've taken you from envisioning the space to the actual construction of your build-out. What could possibly be left? Ah yes—moving you into your new space. How difficult can that be? You simply pick up the *Yellow Pages*, open it to the section on "Movers," select two or three companies, ask for prices and pick the cheapest. It's easy. Oh yeah, make sure you call the company at least two or three weeks before your move.

This doesn't seem right, does it? I've just poured twenty years of experience and an endless amount of research into a step-by-step book on how to avoid the dangers of leasing and now I'm going to touch on the office move? I don't think so. I better find an expert—someone who specializes in commercial and industrial moving.

This wasn't an easy task. Who did I know in the moving and storage industry? No one. What companies have moved tenants of mine in the past? I thought and thought. Finally I picked up the phone, called several of my clients and asked, "Who handled your move and were you satisfied?" The most frequent answer I got was "Hilldrup Moving and Storage, a division of United Van Lines. Talk to Charles Figueroa. He really knows his stuff."

I called Charles and introduced myself. I told him about the book I was writing and how little I knew about the office move. I asked for any information or assistance he might be able to offer. Charles told me he could send me information, but if we were going to do this right, he would prefer to spend some time with me, discussing the office move at length. He had videotapes, brochures and articles he'd be willing to supply, but the move is such an important part of the transaction, it should be discussed in detail.

We spent three hours over lunch discussing the office building industry, the moving and storage industry, market booms, market busts, market trends, large tenants, small tenants, the Chicago office market, the Boston office market, the New York office market and all the Florida office markets. Charles also gave me an article he had written entitled "12 Steps to a Successful Office Move." He gave me permission to use it and since he's the expert when it comes to the office move, here is his article.

Section II. "12 Steps to a Successful Office Move"

The office is moving and you have been charged with the responsibility of choosing the right mover to accomplish this task successfully. "Simple," you say. "I'll just get the phone book and let my fingers do the walking." Wrong! Unfortunately, there's little relationship between the size of a *Yellow Pages'* ad and the quality of service rendered.

The forte of most moving companies is their long-distance household division while their weakest area is commercial moving. An experienced office mover knows that the difference between a residential and a commercial move is as great as the difference between night and day. Yes, they will get you to your new location. But will it be on time, within the budget, and without mishap? Probably not.

Your goal is to accomplish this move as an office hero and not end up the office scapegoat. So instead of playing Russian roulette with the phone book (and your career), ask the building managers at both your present and new locations to recommend two or three moving companies. Property management people have extensive first-hand experience with movers, and are as anxious as you to have the move be a smooth success. Therefore, they are a great place to start your selection process.

Another avenue is to visit your new office building and ask its current tenants which mover they used and the quality of service. Vendors such as your attorney, accountant and insurance agent won't want to jeopardize their relationship with you, so they'll be careful whom they recommend.

After you've selected and pre-qualified potential bidders, take the time to meet individually with each mover's representative for an analysis of the move. Be certain you fully understand what will be done and how the move will be carried out. Estimates from three movers should suffice. However, if it is a large move, you may want to solicit five estimates. Have someone of authority (not just an information gatherer) from your company meet with each mover during the inventory process. Inform the mover about your needs and ask how they propose to meet them. The same representative from your company should meet with all the movers.

During the initial walk-through or inventory process, determine whether you or the mover will be responsible for handling the movement of fragile items such as lamps, paintings and plants. Identify any additional services such as the packing of common areas like the supply room or library, the balancing and bolting of lateral file cabinets, and the disassembly of modular furniture.

After the salesman completes his inventory process, set a time for him to return and make his formal presentation. At that time he should bring a list (with contact names and phone numbers) of the last five companies whose offices his company moved. Tell him not to furnish you with a list of references (which he naturally would pick to create a favorable impression). If your move is very large, request that he provide you with a list of comparable size moves he did in the last twelve months. Ask him to also present at that time his "certificate of insurance" as well as actual pictures of the type of moving equipment he uses. Some movers have been known to simply copy pictures and drawings of equipment they find in other moving company brochures and represent it as their own.

The next step will be to interview your mover. Allow enough time for your mover to make his formal presentation and to answer the following questions:

1.) "What type of moving cartons will you provide?"
The best moving carton folds together and is 1.5 or 2.5 cubic feet in volume. Anything larger is going to be too heavy for your employees to move around during the packing and unpacking stages.

2.) "How will you handle our computers and other electronic equipment?"
The preferred manner is to first wrap each computer component with bubblewrap and then place the protected equipment onto a steel or wooden cart for safe transport. Another method that is very popular is to transport them in a large open box usually made out of cardboard. This is not as safe because they can crush if the load shifts against the box on the truck. Also, since the boxes are open on top, their contents are susceptible to water damage if it rains. The most dangerous method of handling them is to simply blanket wrap them in pads and place them in between the load on the moving van.

166

3.) "How will you handle our lateral file cabinets?"

Moving companies that use the latest state-of-the-art equipment in relocating offices move them without disturbing the contents. There is a new device called a Spider Crane(R) developed for this purpose. With this innovative piece of equipment, the file cabinet is sucked off the floor fully loaded and placed onto a special, low-profile steel dolly. This procedure eliminates the risk of mixed-up or lost files, and gives you 100% access to your files immediately before or after the move. If your mover does not own a Spider Crane(R), they can move them partially-full, providing the cabinet does not have a false bottom and the bottom drawer sits flat on the floor. In this case, you should empty at least the top drawers. However, if the cabinets have false bottoms, the drawers must be completely emptied out.

4.) "How will you handle our desks?"

There is another helpful new invention called Pneumatic Buffers (TM). If your mover owns these special air bags, he can dolly your desk up on end with the contents still in the drawers. By inflating a buffer inside each drawer, the contents are immobilized so that nothing moves or falls out. If your mover does not own Pneumatic Buffers (TM), you must completely empty and pack the contents of all drawers. This is a waste of time and money.

5.) "How will you handle our library?"

Have the mover, under your close supervision, load your books onto book bins, which look like bookcases on wheels. This procedure, like the Spider Crane (R) or the Pneumatic Buffers (TM), greatly reduces your downtime because it gives you 100% access to your books immediately before and after the move. The "Dark Ages method" for moving a library is to pack the books into mountains of boxes where they can easily get mixed up. This system is very labor-intensive and puts you out of business before and after the move.

6.) "How will you protect the office building from being damaged?"

To protect the carpet, masonite sheets should be run down the center of the hallway carpet. To protect the door jambs, clamp a special pad called a door jamb protector to each jamb.

7.) "How will you load the furniture onto the moving van?"

You can immediately measure the level of sophistication of your mover if he uses the "floating" method for loading the furniture, instead of the stacking method. The floating method keeps the furniture on the dolly on the floor of the moving van. It is fast, safe and efficient. The old-fashioned way is the stacking method where the mover un-dollies the furniture onto the truck and stacks it floor to ceiling. This procedure (used on most long-distance household moves) can cause crushing damage to anything at the bottom of the pile. It is also slow and very labor-intensive.

8.) "What provisions do you have for contingencies such as a truck breakdown, elevator failure, or the need for additional men or equipment?"

The best answer is that someone of authority from the moving company will be accessible during your move. Such a person should be the owner or the general manager. Usually a salesman has no decision-making authority in an emergency or last-minute change of strategy.

9.) "What type of insurance coverage do you have?"

If you hire a moving company that does not have adequate insurance and there is an accident on your move, you may be contingently liable. For example, if another tenant's employee is injured during your move (let's say one of your file cabinets falls off a dolly and hits him), the injured tenant might sue you for negligence for hiring a mover without proper coverage. In such a trail of litigation, the one with the insurance often becomes the one who pays.

In another case, if a moving company employee injures himself during the move, you may be liable for his medical expenses and lost wages if your moving company doesn't have workers' compensation insurance. Even worse, your own general liability insurance might exclude such coverage making you directly liable.

If your mover's general liability insurance is inadequate and he causes significant damage to the office building, his insurance may not satisfy the damage claims. Suing him for damages will not necessarily guarantee satisfaction because many movers have a lot of debt and little equity.

For all of these reasons, you must demand a current "certificate of insurance," which lists the workers' compensation coverage as well as the general liability coverage. At a minimum you must require your mover to have statutory limits for workers' compensation and an umbrella policy for $1 million per occurrence.

10.) "Will we be permitted to audit your invoices if we deem it necessary?"

A small minority of movers have a habit of billing for movers who are never on the move (i.e. "ghost movers"). Will his company permit you to examine the payroll and cost records to verify all moving charges if you deem it necessary?

11.) "Can I have a list—including contact names & phone numbers—of the last five office moves your company did?"

After the mover leaves, call all five contacts and ask the following questions:

A.) "When did the mover move you?" Be suspicious if the move occurred more than 6 weeks ago.

B.) "How well did the mover protect your furniture, computers, contents, etc.?"

C.) "How did the mover protect your office against damage?"

D.) "Did the mover complete the job in the time allotted and did their bill exceeded the price quoted?"

12.) Don't attempt to save time by having a "mass walk-through" with all the bidders at one time.

This herd concept has become very popular in recent years, but often undermines the entire selection process. First, movers on a mass walk-through will be afraid to raise vital questions for fear of informing their competitors on how they propose to do the move. The mass walk-through also encourages unrealistically low bids by intimidating those who participate into second guessing their competitor's bids. Finally, the mass walk-through penalizes those movers who are thorough and detailed and subsequently slower in taking their inventory. In order to keep pace with the pack, they are forced to take shortcuts or overlook important details.

If you follow the procedures outlined above, you will have taken a giant step toward being an office hero—congratulated for a job well done—and not the office scapegoat for all the things that went wrong.

This chapter was written, and all the information has been supplied, by Charles Figueroa , Office and Industrial Manager of the Hilldrup Moving & Storage Co., United Van Lines.

CONCLUSION

Leasing office space is complex and could mean life or death for your business. We have all heard stories and seen statistics about the failure rate of small businesses in America. These numbers are devastating. The leading causes of small business failure in this country are poor planning and undercapitalization. The single highest expense for a young company is the cost of office space. It is the most overlooked and lightly addressed issue when most start-up companies prepare their initial business plan.

The ones that plan well have done some research on the cost of office space, but even this research consists of a phone call or two to local buildings to ask for their quoted lease rates. How could you suspect the hidden dangers lurking behind those dollar-per-square-foot quotes? The devastating result of being unprepared could cost you tens of thousands, or even millions of additional dollars, on hidden operating expenses, additional build-out costs, unknown common area factors, or the lure of the low rate that could increase by astronomical proportions over a three- to five-year period.

This book was written to guide you through the proper preparation, research and basic understanding of the office building industry. Through knowledge of the industry's language, methods to research local market conditions, and your ability to identify a landlord's tricks of the trade, the playing field will be leveled. Be aware that you are dealing with people who specialize and make their living in this business. *You are playing in their arena!* Without proper preparation, you are at the mercy of your adversary—the building owner.

I have included a step-by-step chart for you to follow throughout your office leasing transaction. The book and the chart follow the same pattern.

I have found over the years that property owners, whether residential or commercial, have a tendency of dealing in "perceived values" as opposed to "market reality." A property always holds a much higher value to the seller/owner than it does to the prospective buyer. Once the prospective buyer becomes the owner, the property's value tends to skyrocket. This theory is especially true when applied to building owners as they set their lease rates or selling price.

The market always dictates the property's true value. "Supply and demand" can be the property owner and prospective tenant's best friend—or worst enemy. The key is understanding it and taking advantage of it.

The office building industry is based on profit and survival. It's quite similar to the law of the jungle: "Only the strong survive." Unfortunately, "the strong" in this industry are rarely the nice guys and gals. In this industry, people understand that in order to survive, they must constantly find ways to stay profitable. If the market is strong, they raise rents and give little in negotiations. If the market is weak, they may reduce or maintain rates—appearing to give a lot in negotiations—but turn profits by hiding additional costs in subtle but tricky or repetitive lease clauses. Some owners may even cut the quality of service or reduce their level of building maintenance.

It is not my intent to paint a picture of all owners or landlords as evil people. Most of them are not. And, everyone has the right to make a profit.

However, it is my intention to protect you—the consumer— by exposing the hidden profits, "the tricks of the trade." If the building owner has the right to make a profit, you certainly have an equal right to know how much you're actually paying for his product.

The information and methods I have shared with you are proven. Over the years they have saved my clients millions of dollars. To hire me as a consultant, speaker or instructor please call 1-800-699-4901.

VISUALIZE	PREPARE	DETERMINE	CONTACT	SEARCH	SELECT	NEGOTIATE	FINALIZE
1) Invision your space	1) Learn Market terminology	1) Space Preference: a. New Space b. Re-new current space c. Sub-lease	1) Broker (if so)	1) Touring the buildings a. Ask questions b. Look hard	1) Request Proposal	1) Negotiate the Proposal	1) Negotiate Legal Points
2) Determine your needs	2) Prepare your market study	2) Do I need a broker?	2) Preliminary Tour a. Drive-by b. Walk-thru	2) Narrow your choice to 3	2) Site for space-plan	2) Review pricing of construction of space	2) Neutralize lease
	3) Requirements: a. Square feet b. Budget c. Location d. Style Bldg.		3) Phone for info.		3) Present financials if	3) Adjust Space-plan	3) Negotiate Final BSNS points
	4) Have financial info on co. ready		4) Set appointments		4) Receive & review the proposal	4) Ask for a copy of the lease	4) Confirm all plans & pricing
						5) Send lease to atty. for legal review	5) Sign lease & attached documents
							6) Await return of signed lease
							7) Check on buildout
							8) Final space walk-thru
							9) Move in

174

GLOSSARY OF TERMS

Abatement. A reduction or decrease; usually referred to in terms of rent or other increases.

Above Building Standard. Typically refers to items not included in the construction work letter. The work letter indicates what the ownership of the building will include in a standard office build-out.

Absorbed Space. Represents the net change of the amount of office space in a given period of time.

Absorption Rate. The percentage of space in a market either taken off the market or added back into the pool of existing office space. Typically, a gain in market absorption represents space that is now leased, that was not previously leased; or in a negative absorbed market space that was leased, that's now vacant.

Absorption Period. The amount of time given to lease or sell a given amount of space.

Addendum. A document containing any additions or changes negotiated in the original lease. This document is always attached to the signed lease and is part of the lease. Items addressed in an addendum supersede the item being replaced in the lease.

Add-On Factor. Also referred to as a loss factor, common area factor or core factor. The areas of a structure that are common to all tenants in the building, such as restrooms, corridors, storage rooms, electrical rooms, janitorial closets, lobbies, etc.

Ad Valorem. This is a term typically used when referring to property taxes that are assessed by the government according to their valuation of the property.

After-Hours Usage. Tenant's need for additional working hours beyond the normal operating hours for the building as set forth in the lease. Typically, if the tenant requires after-hour utility usage, he or she will pay an additional agreed-upon fee.

Amenities. Attractive features of a property such as a coffee shop, health facility, conference rooms, covered parking, etc.

Amendment. A document negotiated after the original lease is in effect that changes or adds items to the original lease. This document is to be attached to the signed original lease and becomes part of the lease. Items addressed in an amendment supersede the item being replaced in the original lease document.

Americans with Disabilities Act (ADA). Federal legislation passed in 1990 that requires employees and business owners to make reasonable accommodations to facilitate employment of the disabled.

Amortization. Represents periodic payments of principal and interest to be paid back over the term of a loan.

Annual Bumps. Slang for annual increases in such items as rent or operating expense increases.

Annual Operating Expense Increases/Overages. A charge passed onto the tenant representing the tenant's proportionate share of building operating expense costs greater than the amount agreed upon in the original lease (referred to in lease as "expense stop" or "base year expenses"). When the owner refers to the building's "expense stop" as $4.50, this simply means that the first $4.50 of building operating expenses are being paid by the building. If the building operates at a higher rate— let's say $5 per square foot—the tenant pays the difference between $5 and $4.50, or an additional 50 cents per square foot.

When an owner quotes a "base year basis," he is saying the tenant will pay the difference between the amount the building operated at in the base year addressed in the lease and the current operating expense cost. An example would be "base year of 1995." Let's say the building operated at $6 per square foot in 1995 and operates at $6.50 in 1996. The tenant would pay the difference of 50 cents per square foot in 1996.

Annual Rental Rate. The cost per square foot that the landlord is quoting or receiving in rent (i.e. $14 per square foot. Sometimes quoted in annual dollar amounts: $14,000 per year).

Appraisal. The estimation of an opinion of value given on a property. An appraisal of property is to be based on factual information given by a qualified professional appraiser.

Appreciation. An increase in the value of the property.

Assessment. The estimated value of property in order for a governmental fee to be imposed, such as taxes or area improvements.

Assignment of Lease. The transfer of all responsibilities and liabilities of the lease from one party to another.

Attornment. The turning over of items of value, such as money or property, to a new owner.

Audit. The inspection of records to assure accuracy.

Base Rent. The rental rate at commencement of the lease. It is subject to annual increases unless otherwise negotiated in the lease, addendum, or amendment. This phrase has more than one meaning. To some landlords and in some markets it refers to the rental rate minus operating expenses. For example: $14 per square foot quoted rate. The building operates at $6.50 (operating expense cost); therefore, the base rate (net rent) is $7.50.

Base Year Operating Expenses. The amount the owner is paying to cover the cost of operating the building in a given year. For example, "base year 1995 expenses" would reflect the cost to operate the subject building in 1995. In subsequent years the tenant would pay the difference in the amount it costs to operate the building, based on the percentage of the building they occupy.

Bay Depth. Represents the distance from the building's corridor wall to the outside window of the building.

BOMA (Building Owners & Managers Association). An international organization made up of building owners, building managers and suppliers of the same. Because of its size and influence, the organization establishes a variety of recommended guidelines, such as the "BOMA method of measurement."

BOMA Method of Measurement. Generally accepted throughout the office building industry as the standard and fair method of measuring office space. Some landlords use other methods, including their own. To determine the "usable area" of your space, you must measure from the inside finished surface of the corridor wall and the dominant portion of other permanent walls (dominant portion of exterior walls, i.e. could be glass) to the center of the wall that separates your office from the adjoining office.

Columns and interior walls should not be deducted from the measurement. To determine the "rentable area" of your space, you must first determine the rentable area of your floor. This would be accomplished by measuring the inside finished surfaces of the outer building (might be outer glass to outer glass that makes up the exterior walls of the floor). Remember— Length multiplied by Width = Square Footage.

When measuring, exclude any "vertical penetrations" such as stairwells, elevator shafts, flues, vertical ducting, etc., before you determine the usable area of that floor. This would be accomplished by taking the rentable measurement and subtracting areas of common use to the tenant (i.e. corridors, restrooms, utility closets, janitorial closets, and building amenities located on that floor, such as a common conference room.)

To determine your "rentable area," "usable area" and "common area factors," apply the following conversion formulas:

Rentable Area divided by Usable Area = Rentable/Usable Ratio

Usable Area multiplied by Rentable/Usable Ratio = Rentable Area

Rentable Area divided by Rentable/Usable Ratio = Usable Area

Broker. One who acts as an intermediary between landlord and prospective tenant. A broker could be acting on behalf of the tenant (tenant representative), or the landlord (building representative). The broker is generally paid by the landlord, unless other financial arrangements have been made, or the broker's registration of the prospective tenant has been rejected by the landlord.

Building Amenities. Features of the building that add to the comfort of the tenants (i.e. coffee shop, health facility, covered parking, breakrooms, conference rooms, express mail machines, etc.).

Building Codes. A set of laws enacted by local government to regulate the operation of office buildings within its jurisdiction.

Building Improvements. Any improvements made to the overall appearance or comfort of the building (i.e. new carpeting, painting, upgrade of elevator cabs, etc.).

Building Operating Hours. The normal hours of operation for the building as set forth in the lease.

Building Standard. Refers to the items covered in the construction work letter defining the items necessary to create a standard office space.

Build-Out. Refers to the construction of the tenant's proposed space to make it ready for occupancy. Or, to comply with tenant's construction needs according to the terms and conditions of the lease. Also referred to as "T.I." (tenant improvements).

Build to Suit. The build-out of space according to the tenant's established guidelines.

Buy Out. The ability to pay money or something of value in order to be released from the obligations of a lease.

Cash Flow. The amount of money the landlord will receive from the lease after the deduction of operating expenses, taxes and insurance.

Certificate of Occupancy. A document issued by local government stating the office space is in proper condition and can be occupied.

Change Order. A document usually signed by the tenant when making a revision to the original build-out plans. It represents the tenant's authorization to revise and usually indicates the tenant's willingness to pay for the revision.

Class A Building. A term commonly used when referring to the highest quality buildings. Building classification may rate how the building is generally accepted in the market, or could be a personal classification by the individual referring to that structure.

Class B Building. A term commonly used to describe an average building. Building classification may rate how the building is generally accepted in the market, or could be a personal classification by the individual referring to that structure.

Class C Building. A term commonly used to describe a below-average building. Building classification may rate how the building is generally accepted in the market, or could be a personal classification by the individual referring to that structure.

Commencement Date. Date the lease takes effect. Usually from the landlord's perspective; the day the tenant starts paying rent on the occupied space.

Commission. A fee generally paid to a real estate broker, or other properly licensed individual, for acting as the procuring cause of the transaction.

Common Area. Any space in a building affording common use for all tenants. For example: lobbies, corridors, restrooms, building breakrooms, building conference room, health facility, janitorial closets and storage rooms. It does not include vertical penetrations such as stairwells, elevator shafts, flues or vertical ducting.

Common Area Factor. A percentage of the building determined by the building owner to represent the total amount of space in the building affording common use for all tenants such as lobbies, corridors, restrooms, building breakrooms, building conference rooms, health facility, janitorial closets and storage rooms. This excludes "vertical penetrations" such as stairwells and elevator shafts.

Common Area Maintenance Fees (CAM Recovery). In retail, a fee charged to tenants to maintain the outward and overall appearance of the property. In the office building industry, a generally interchangeable term with "overage of operating expenses."

Comparables. Properties similar to a particular property; used as a comparison to determine a fair market value.

Concession. Item(s) given up during negotiations. Coming from the landlord, it could be in the form of free rent or other reductions. From a tenant, it could be backing off on a demand.

Condemnation. The process in which the government is able to take property from an owner without the owner's consent. Also referred to as "eminent domain"—they do not have to get the owner's consent, and the owner is compensated for the property.

CPI (Consumer Price Index). In most leases this is used as the basis for adjusting annual rent increases. It is also referred to as a "cost of living increase." CPI is the federal government index that measures the change in cost of a variety of goods. It is used as an indicator to reflect future pricing as an adjustment for inflation.

Contiguous Space. Refers to the space next door or adjoining the tenant's occupied space.

Contract Rent. The actual rent paid under the terms of the lease.

Conveyance. The transfer of title or ownership from one party to another.

Covenant. A promise or assurance given by one party to another. Another definition is "a legal restriction of property."

Date of Lease. The date the lease has been executed by both tenant and landlord.

Debt Service. Payments made on a loan.

Deed. A document that proves ownership.

Default. Non-performance under the terms of the lease.

Demising Wall. A common wall that separates two tenants. (Usually to the underside of the floor above.)

Depreciation. A decrease in property value.

Dominant Portion. A feature that makes up more than 50% of the inside surface of a permanent wall.

Easement. The right given to another party to either use a portion of the property or to cross the property freely.

Economic Rent. An analysis used to determine the property's market rent.

Effective Rate. Overall average of the tenant's rate taken through the entire term of occupancy. Takes into effect annual increases. For example: a rate quoted at $14 per square foot—on a five-year deal with annual increases of 4%—would be effectively a $15.17 deal.

Efficiency. A term used when describing the building's common area factor; sometimes used to describe how well the building is being run as reflected in lower operating expenses.

Electrical or Utilities. When referred to in a lease, reflects a cost that is either being paid separately by the tenant under a net or triple net lease, or a cost that is included under the full-service or gross lease.

Eminent Domain. A method used by the government to acquire property by condemnation. They do not have to get the owner's consent, and the owner is compensated for the property.

Encroachment. Refers typically to a property use or structure that extends over someone else's property line.

Encumberance. A claim or lien filed against a property.

Equity. When referred to in conjunction with commercial property it usually refers to one's ownership position in the property.

Equity Participation. The participation by the lender in an active ownership position with the property.

Escalation Clause. Addresses the increases to be passed onto the tenant during the life of the lease.

Estoppel Certificate. Document signed by the tenant stating the current condition of the lease and any other agreements between the landlord and tenant.

Escrow Agreement. Governs the terms under which money is placed into an escrow account and how it is to be handled or distributed.

Exclusive Agreement. An agreement between an owner and a brokerage firm stating that the broker will be the sole representative in marketing the property for sale or lease or to manage this property. In return the owner promises to compensate the broker by paying a commission or a fee, according to the terms and conditions of this agreement.

Executive Office Suites or Central Secretarial Services. These are usually one, two or several small offices. An executive office suite operation is usually operated by a company leasing space within a building and subleasing small portions of their leased space to sub-tenants. On occasion you will find the landlord running such an operation within his or her own building, to encourage these firms to grow within the same building. This type of firm offer companies not only a local office presence but also the typical office services, i.e. secretarial, telephone answering, meeting rooms, faxing, typing, copying, etc., necessary to support their business operation, without going to the expense or bother of hiring their own staff. When leasing an office in such an operation be aware that pricing is based on the sale of their services, not the cost of office space. For instance you may lease 125 sq. ft. room from the xyz Company, at a rate three or four times the rate being quoted for office space rental in the same building.

Exhibit. An attachment to the lease.

Expansion. Refers to the transaction involved for a tenant to add additional space to his existing office space.

Expense Stop. An established dollar amount toward operating expenses of the building that the landlord is willing to pay. The tenant will be required to pay his or her proportionate share of any costs over and above this set amount.

Face Rent. The asking rent.

Fair Market Value. The price the property would most likely bring in the current market.

Fiduciary. Loyalty to a certain party.

Finished Surface. A wall, ceiling or floor, including glass, that's been placed in the space for the tenant's use.

First Right of Refusal. A right given to the tenant stating that before the landlord will lease the space in question (usually expansion space), the tenant will be given the right to lease it first.

Fixed Costs. Costs that remain constant.

Flex Space. Sometimes referred to as office/showroom space. It consists of some office but mostly warehouse space.

Floor Load Capacity. The amount of weight a floor in a building is safely capable of sustaining, per square inch.

Force Majeure. Natural act(s) of God.

Free Rent. A period of time given to the tenant by the landlord to occupy the space before having to commence paying rent. Usually done during extreme soft periods in leasing when the market is known as a "tenant's market."

Full-Service Lease. In some markets referred to as a "gross lease" and is meant to cover the cost of rent, electricity and janitorial service. Does not include phones, furniture, moving, etc. [BEWARE: Sometimes this term is used when referring to a "modified gross lease."]

Functional Design. A plan affording a tenant maximum efficiency of their space.

General Contractor. The individual or company that coordinates all construction work, oversees the construction, and hires and is responsible to pay all subcontractors.

Graduated Lease. A lease with varied rental payments; sometimes referred to as a "stepped lease."

Gross Lease. A lease that is all-inclusive. The tenant pays rent and the owner pays all expenses related to the property.

Gross Square Footage. Total square footage of the building or property.

Guarantee. If a business is relatively new (under five years), its financial statement is not very strong. Thus, the landlord may have some discomfort with the prospective tenant's ability to last through the lease and might ask for a personal or corporate guarantee. It is assurance that if the tenant defaults, the person or entity guaranteeing the lease will pay rent and continue to live up to all the terms and conditions of the lease.

Holding Over. A tenant remains in their space beyond the agreed-upon term of the lease.

HVAC. Refers to heating, air-conditioning and other ventilation systems within the building.

Improvements. Usually refers to construction being done within the tenant's space or within the building itself.

Indirect Costs. Typically, support costs such as administrative, financing or property taxes, as opposed to costs such as direct labor or direct purchase of materials for the tenant's use.

Inventory. Amount of space available within a given market.

Janitorial. An expense generally covered under a full-service lease, and paid for under the terms of a net or triple net lease arrangement. Normal janitorial functions typically include light dusting, emptying of trash and ashtrays, and light cleaning or vacuuming of floors.

Landlord. The person who controls, operates, or owns the property.

Landlord's Lease. A lease written and weighed to the advantage of the landlord.

Landlord's Market. An office market showing strong signs of being favorable to the landlord. Typically a market that's experiencing strong leasing activity, and doesn't have a lot of available space.

Landlord's Warrant. This gives the landlord the right to lien a tenant's personal property and the right to sell it to collect delinquent rent.

Lease. The legal agreement between the landlord and tenant setting forth the rules and conditions for occupancy by the tenant and limitations of the landlord.

Leasable Square Footage. The amount of space in the building, or within the tenant's space, once the common area or load factor has been added to the usable measurement. It is typically the amount of square footage the tenant's rental rate is based on.

Usable Square Footage + Load Factor = Leasable Square Footage

Lease Commencement Date. The date the lease begins.

Lease Expiration. The date when the lease expires, according to the terms and conditions set forth in the lease.

Lease Extension. An agreed-upon period of time between landlord and tenant that the lease term can be extended.

Lease Proposal. A presentation, usually written, of the proposed lease terms and conditions for the prospective tenant's occupancy.

Lease Term. Number of months or years the agreed-upon lease will remain in force.

Leasee. The individual or company leasing space from another party.

Leasing Agent. The individual assigned the responsibility, usually by the building owner, to lease out the property.

Lessor. The individual or building owner leasing space to another party.

Letter of Credit. A pledge or a commitment made by a lender or other party at the request of a party to honor drafts or any other payment.

Letter of Intent. A lease proposal with an acceptance signature block for both parties. It may or may not be legally binding, depending on the statements in the agreement.

Lien. An encumberance against personal items such as property for money.

Listing Agreement. An agreement between a property owner and a broker giving the broker the right to sell or lease the owner's property in return for compensation.

Load Factor or Loss Factor. The difference between "rentable" and "usable" square footage in a building. Also referred to as "common area factor."

Maintenance. Care and upkeep of the property.

Management. Oversees the day-to-day operations of the office building.

Market Analysis. A study reflecting various conditions of a given market.

Market Indicators. Statistical data pinpointing particular reasons for effect on a market.

Market Rate. Price that is generally acceptable for a particular product within a given market.

Market Rent. The amount of rent the property would most likely attain on the open market.

Market Survey. A study of vital statistics from various properties effecting a segment of the market.

Mixed-Use Building. Also referred to as a multi-tenant building. Tenancy is made up of more than one tenant in various businesses.

Modified Gross Lease. A type of lease where the tenant pays rent and included are all costs related to the operation of the building, except the tenant pays his or her proportionate share of operating expense overages.

Month-to-Month Lease. An agreement by landlord and tenant to allow the tenant to occupy space on a month-to-month basis. Typically this type of lease can be terminated by either party with a thirty-day notice.

Monthly Rent. One-twelfth of the annual rent paid to the landlord usually on the first of the month.

Multi-Tenant Building. A building that houses more than one tenant.

Multi-Tenant Floor. A floor that houses more than one tenant.

Net Lease. A lease that is not all-inclusive. For example: the lease states the tenant will pay for his own janitorial or electrical service; or the lease states the tenant will pay separately for both janitorial and utilities.

Net Operating Income. The amount of money left after deducting operating expenses, taxes and insurance from the building's gross income.

Net Present Value (NPV). The value of the lease once all costs of doing a transaction are deducted from the gross income of a lease.

Net Rentable Area. The measurement of a space, floor or building minus all vertical penetrations. This term is also referred to as "usable."

Non-Competitive Clause. Restricts the landlord from leasing space to a business that's similar or competitive to the existing tenant.

Non-Disturbance Clause. Insures the tenant quiet enjoyment while occupying his or her office space.

Normal Use. Tenant will use the premises for permitted purposes within the guidelines of the lease, during normal building operating hours.

Open Space Plan. An office design that eliminates walls.

Operating Expenses. The landlord's cost to operate the property. Some items included are real estate taxes and assessments, other taxes, utilities, insurance, maintenance and repairs, common area refurbishing, janitorial, materials and supplies, repair services, cost of property management, security fees, employees and contractors, outside maintenance, cost of signs, rubbish removal, pest control, bulb replacement, etc.

Operating Expense Pass-Throughs. The amount that is passed onto the tenant in order to operate the building. This would represent any amount over and above the amount agreed to in the lease, referred to as "base year expenses" or the "expense stop." This amount would be proportionate to the percentage of space occupied by the tenant in the building.

Operating Expense Stop. Is a method used by the Landlord for passing building operating expenses on to the Tenant (An additional charge). It is a dollar amount established by the Landlord to indicate how much of the actual building operating expenses will be included or covered by your rental rate. For instance if you are quoted a lease rate of $14 per square foot with an expense stop of $4.00, your rental rate is actually $10 and the additional $4 of the quoted $14 per square foot will cover the first $4 of your proportionate share of operating expenses. Let's say the above building's actual operating expenses are $7.60, because your expense stop is $4.00 you will be expected to pay an additional $3.00 per square foot to make up the diffence between your quoted expense stop and the building's actual operating expenses. In reality you are living with a $17.00 per square foot first year rate (including operating expenses). Remember the building's operating expenses usually increase annually.

Option. A clause in the lease that gives the tenant some future right in the lease.

Pass-Throughs. Building and operating expenses paid by the tenant.

Percentage Lease. Generally used for retail leases in which rent is based on a percentage of sales.

Pre-Leasing. The leasing of a project before construction of the project has been completed.

Pro Rata Share. Percentage of building occupied by the tenant, which is usually based on the rentable or leasable square footage measurement of tenant space compared to the rentable or leasable square footage of the building.

Proration. A division of cost proportionately based on a given period of time.

Quoted Rate. The rate per square foot that is quoted to prospective tenants when inquiring about the property. May or may not be negotiable. This may be quoted on a rentable or usable basis.

Reassessment. Re-evaluating the value of a property.

Relocation Clause. Gives landlord the right to move the tenant within the building and during the lease period.

Rehab. Reconstruction of a building or a space to bring it up to date.

Renewal. Remaining in your present space by being allowed to renew your lease for a period of time.

Renewal Option. Gives the tenant the right to renew their lease, under certain terms and conditions, and usually within a certain given time frame.

Rent. Money or something of value paid from tenant to landlord for the right to occupy space in the landlord's property.

Rentable Square Footage. The amount of square feet, including the common area factor of the building. This typically is the square footage the tenant will pay rent on.

Rent Commencement Date. The date the tenant begins paying rent.

Rental Rate. The agreed-upon rate that space is leased at.

Rent Roll. A list of tenants occupying space in the building.

Security Deposit. An amount of the tenant's money, usually placed in escrow, insuring the landlord that all obligations of the lease will be met and the office space will not be damaged.

Single-Floor Tenancy. A entire floor occupied by a single tenant.

Space Plan. A drawing that represents the tenant's build-out requirements within the desired office space.

Space Planner. One who draws and designs the space plan, usually an architect.

Spec Space. Office space built out prior to being leased to a particular tenant. The space is considered speculative in nature.

Sublease. Occurs when a tenant re-leases their space during the term of their tenancy. It is generally a three-party transaction. Subleasee leases space from tenant and landlord approves.

Tenant. An individual or company that occupies space under the terms and conditions of a lease document.

Tenant-at-Sufferance. A tenant who has stayed beyond the termination of their lease.

Tenant-at-Will. A tenant who holds occupancy for an unknown amount of time. Usually has the landlord's approval.

Tenant Improvements. Usually refers to the improvements to be done to a space to make it ready for the new tenant's occupancy. It can also mean improvements being done by a tenant.

Tenant Improvement Allowance. The amount of money the landlord is willing to contribute for the build-out of the tenant's space. Usually quoted as "x" amount of dollars per rentable or usable square feet.

Tenant Eviction. Landlord sues to remove tenant from the leased premises, usually due to non-payment or non-conformity to the rules and regulations of the property.

Tenant's Lease. Any lease giving the tenant more rights than the landlord.

Tenant's Market. Normally a weak market. Slow leasing activity and lots of space available throughout the entire market.

Tenant Representative. Any broker or representative exclusively representing the rights of a tenant during the course of a transaction.

Tenant's Services. Those services provided to the tenant by the landlord under the terms and conditions of the lease.

Triple Net Lease. A lease in which the tenant pays all expenses, including their rent.

Turn-Key Build-Out. A completed build-out of space ready for the tenant to move into.

Unencumbered. Free of liens, or free and clear.

Usable Square Footage. The amount of square feet measured within the confines of the tenant's space, no add-ons.

Use. Purpose of occupancy.

Vacancy Factor. The amount of space not occupied in the building.

Vertical Penetrations. Areas serving more than one tenant such as stairwells, elevator shafts, flues, pipe shafts and vertical ducts. For measurement purposes these items are not deducted if they serve a single tenant.

Warranty. When used in conjunction with a lease or an office property a warranty gives certain assurances from the seller to the buyer or from the building owner to the tenant.

Wear and Tear. Deterioration of space due to occupancy.

Wet Column. A column through which plumbing can be accessed for installation of sinks, drinking fountains, etc.

Working Drawings. The plans from which the contractor will build a tenant's office space. These are also the plans that have received governmental approval during the permitting process.

Work Letter. Usually an attachment to the lease that indicates the materials considered building standard for the build-out of a tenant's office space. Includes the amount of money the landlord is willing to contribute toward the build-out.

Zoning. Governmentally-regulated uses of a certain area or building. Zoning controls the type of businesses that can operate within an area.

Zoning Ordinance. The set of laws set up by the local government for the control of uses of property within the community.

INDEX

199

M

203

Z

Please send me _____ Free report(s) on leasing Executive Office Suites

Please send me _____ copies of OFFICE SPACE: A Tenant's Guide To Profitable Leasing.

Enclosed is a _____Check/Money Order

Please charge my ☐ VISA ☐ MasterCard ☐ American Express

Card No._____ Expiration Date _____

Signature _____

Please send book(s) to:

Name _____

Company _____

Address _____

City/State/Zip _____

Phone: _____ Fax _____

To Order Call: **(800) 699-4901**

or Fax order to: **(407) 699-4948**

Make Checks Payable to: **Jack Saltman**

(allow 6 to 8 weeks for delivery)

Mail to or Write: **Jack Saltman**
P.O. Box 940658
Maitland, Florida 32794-0658

Qty	Unit price	Total
		$
	FL Resid. Sales Tax	$
	Shipping & Handling	$3.95
	Total	

Please send me _____ Free report(s) on leasing Executive Office Suites

Please send me _____ copies of OFFICE SPACE: A Tenant's Guide To Profitable Leasing.

Enclosed is a _____Check/Money Order

Please charge my ☐ VISA ☐ MasterCard ☐ American Express

Card No._____ Expiration Date _____

Signature _____

Please send book(s) to:

Name _____

Company _____

Address _____

City/State/Zip _____

Phone: _____ Fax _____

To Order Call: **(800) 699-4901**

or Fax order to: **(407) 699-4948**

Make Checks Payable to: **Jack Saltman**

(allow 6 to 8 weeks for delivery)

Mail to or Write: **Jack Saltman**
P.O. Box 940658
Maitland, Florida 32794-0658

Qty	Unit price	Total
		$
	FL Resid. Sales Tax	$
	Shipping & Handling	$3.95
	Total	